TO MY
PEOPLE
WITH LOVE

John Killinger

To My People with Love

The Ten Commandments for Today

Abingdon Press

Nashville

To My People with Love: The Ten Commandments for Today

Copyright © 1988 by Abingdon Press

Library of Congress Cataloging-in-Publication Data

Killinger, John.
  To my people with love.

  1. Ten commandments. I. Title.
BV4655.K55   1988   241.5'2   88-10518
ISBN 0-687-42200-0 (pubk. : alk. paper)

This book is printed on acid-free paper.

Scripture quotations in this publication, unless otherwise noted are from the Revised Standard Version of the Bible, copyrighted 1946, 1952, © 1971, 1973 by the Division of Christian Education of the National Council of the Churches of Christ in the U.S.A., and are used by permission.

Scripture quotations marked JBP are from *The New Testament in Modern English*, Revised Edition. Copyright © J. B. Phillips, 1958, 1959, 1960, 1972. Reprinted by permission.

Scripture quotations marked NEB are from *The New English Bible.* © The Delegates of the Oxford University Press and The Syndics of the Cambridge University Press 1961, 1970. Reprinted by permission.

Excerpts from *The Dream* by Keith Miller Copyright © 1985 by Word Books. Used by permission.

Excerpts from "The War Within: An Anatomy of Lust" Copyright © 1982 by LEADERSHIP. Used by permission.

MANUFACTURED BY THE PARTHENON PRESS AT
NASHVILLE, TENNESSEE, UNITED STATES OF AMERICA

To David and Betty Harkness,
friends for years,
with love and best wishes

Contents

Foreword

You were probably shocked, as I was, by a national news report that compared the top seven problems reported by schools in 1940 and in 1987. In 1940, the problems were talking out of turn, chewing gum, making noise, running in the halls, cutting in line, dress code infractions, and loitering. In 1987, the list had changed to include drug and alcohol abuse, pregnancy, suicide, rape, robbery, and assault.

This report was shocking, but it was not surprising. Everyone knows that our world has become the locus of almost incredible disorder, crime, terror, and distress. Many ordinary citizens now live behind locks and bars, virtual prisoners in their own homes. Young children are exposed regularly to obscenity, violence, drugs, pornography, and sexual experiences. Family life is in a shambles. The marketplace seethes with greed, corruption, and cutthroat competition. Our legal system has become so entangled and undependable that it usually imposes more hardship on the innocent than on the guilty. Government grows more and more expensive and unwieldy; yet it is less and less responsive to human need. Even religion has borne its share of sexual and financial scandals, and churches often seem insensitive to the widespread sufferings of humanity.

What has gone wrong with the world? What has happened to the days when the streets were safe, schools were temples, and the only drugs in town were dispensed at the village pharmacy? When did we reach the point where everything was out of control and the future began to spell disaster instead of hope?

There are no easy answers, but surely part of the problem is the loss of faith and the growing secularization of society. When millions of people are crammed together in urban areas without the structural advantage of a shared belief in God and life-styles derived from that belief, we shouldn't expect them to get along as if they were all on a Sunday school outing. The weakening of mainline religion in America, together with the influx of great numbers of people from nonchristian cultures, has made us particularly vulnerable to what Amos Wilder once called "the acids of modernity."

It is time we took seriously again the social dimensions of religious commitment and understood for ourselves, as we have for ancient civilizations, the consequences of abandoning our spiritual heritage. Unless we rediscover the Law of God and its role in our society, then we are condemning ourselves by default to live by the law of the jungle.

John Killinger

The Key to a Good Life:

The Real Story of The Ten Commandments

The Ten Commandments. For many of us, the very words denote harshness and repression.

We are like the boy who was practicing his knot-tying with a friend in the Boy Scout room of the church basement. In the course of his practice, he produced a strange looking knot neither of them had ever seen before. "Look," he said, "I've invented a new knot!"

"What are you going to call it?" asked his friend.

He thought for a moment. Then, remembering where they were, he responded: "The Thou Shalt Knot!"

So often we think of the commandments as a list of "thou shalt nots." They hem us in and restrict our freedom. Our reaction to them is mainly negative. Even if we aren't guilty, they evoke a sense of guilt in us.

A Roman Catholic priest once told me about some of the strange confessions he had heard. Two of his favorites were from small boys, one of them eight and the other ten. Each of them, at separate times, had confessed to having committed adultery.

"In neither case," the priest said, "could I believe that the little fellow sitting there in the confessional had committed adultery. So I continued, gently probing, to see what they had really done."

"Would you believe it?" he said. "One had been in a peeing contest and the other had been looking at the ladies' underwear section of the Sears catalog!"

For them, the church had unfortunately become associated with moralism, with acceptance based on a certain code of behavior, and the Ten Commandments lay behind the association.

Are the commandments really negative? Did God give them to the ancient Hebrews as an affliction, as a burden to bear? This isn't the impression we get when we read the story of the commandments in the book of Exodus. There, in the midst of high drama, the people of Israel stood around the foot of Mt. Sinai in a thunderstorm. When Moses went up into the clouds to meet with their God named Yahweh, the commandments were bestowed as a blessing. They were given to constitute a bond between Yahweh and his people.

"I am the Lord your God," says Yahweh,"who brought you out of the land of Egypt, out of the house of bondage" (Exodus 20:2). This is the signature on the commandments. They are a gift from the mighty One who has saved the Israelites from slavery. If the Israelites lived by the commandments, things would go well for them. If they didn't, they would fare poorly.

The commandments are not mere moral imperatives, intended to shackle people to arbitrary burdens. They are the rules of life itself, and anyone who follows them will experience freedom and joy.

There is something about most of us, of course, that doesn't like rules. We are instinctively rebellious, like the little tomboy sitting on the front porch sulking when her daddy came home from work.

"What's wrong with Puddin'?" he asked his wife.

"Oh," said his wife, "she just found out that there's a law of gravity, and she's mad about it."

There are rules in the moral universe that are fully as real and important to know as the rules of the physical universe. The created order is not entirely chaotic and unpredictable. The better we know and observe the rules, the more they will work for us to produce favorable consequences. I cannot leap off the housetop without running counter to the law of gravity and risking serious injury. By the same token I cannot disregard God, kill another human being, or commit adultery without going against the moral nature of things and hurting myself.

When God gave the Israelites the Ten Commandments, he was saying, in essence, "I love you. Look what I've done for you already. Now I want to give you something wonderful, which will help you to live joyfully and productively in the land I'm going to give you. Here are these sayings. Learn them and live by them. They will bless your lives."

In her beautiful novel about Maine, *The Country of the Pointed Firs*, Sara Orne Jewett describes the ascent of a woman writer on the pathway leading to the home of a retired sea captain named Elijah Tilley. On the way, the woman notes a number of wooden stakes scattered about the property in random fashion, with no discernible order. Each is painted white and trimmed in yellow, like the captain's house. Curious, she asks Captain Tilley what they mean. When he first plowed the ground, he says, his plow snagged on many large rocks just beneath the surface. So he set out the stakes where the rocks lay in order to avoid them in the future.

In a sense, this is what God has done with the Ten Commandments. He has set out the stakes where the rocks are. He has said, "These are the trouble spots in life. Avoid these, and you won't snag your plow."

Viewed in this light, we can understand why the ancient Hebrews were so proud of the commandments, why they inscribed them on bits of parchment and sewed them into the sleeves of their garments or wore them in bands around their heads. We can appreciate the enthusiasm of the psalmist:

> Blessed is the man
> who walks not in the counsel of
> the wicked,
> nor stands in the way of sinners,
> nor sits in the seat of scoffers;
> but his delight is in the law of the
> Lord,
> and on his law he meditates day
> and night.
> He is like a tree

14

planted by streams of water,
that yields its fruit in its season,
and its leaf does not wither.
In all that he does, he prospers.

(Psalm 1:1-3)

"Oh, how I love thy law!" exclaims another psalm.

It is my meditation all the day. . . .
How sweet are thy words to my
taste,
sweeter than honey to my mouth! . . .
Thy word is a lamp to my feet
and a light to my path.

(Psalm 119:97, 103, 105)

"But what about Christ?" someone may ask. "Didn't he do away with the Law? Aren't we under grace today, and not under the Law?"

It is true that law and grace are opposites in our vocabularies. We remember that Jesus frequently opposed the scribes and Pharisees, who were the sworn defenders of the Law in his day. We are the heirs of the teaching of the apostle Paul, especially in Romans and Galatians, that the Law can become an instrument of sin, binding burdens that are impossible to bear, and that only the grace of God is able to save us for eternity. We still get goose bumps at the war cry of the Reformation, "Salvation by grace alone!"

But we need to go back and restudy the Gospels to see that Jesus never rejected the Law. Our only

15

glimpse of him as a young man is the picture of him as a youthful scholar of the Law, arguing with the learned doctors in the Temple. It was the thoroughness with which he knew and loved the Law that enabled him to argue so effectively with the scribes and Pharisees. His confrontation with them was not over the Law's existence but over its interpretation.

He held the view expressed by Moshe, the divinely mad prophet in Elie Wiesel's *The Oath*. Azriel, the narrator of the story, was speaking with his friend Moshe one evening after a Hasidic meeting. Moshe asked Azriel:

"You go to school?"
"Of course."
"To what purpose?"
"To learn."
"Learn what?"
"Torah," [Azriel] said, growing uneasy.
"Torah is life, and life must be lived; it cannot be learned from books, between four walls."
"I thought," [Azriel] said, "that Torah is more than life, since God Himself submits to its commandments . . . "
"God too must be lived, my boy. You must live Him, not study Him in books, between four walls!" (Elie Wiesel, *The Oath* [New York: Schocken Books, 1986], p. 120)

Jesus saw better than anyone the mistake of turning the Law into an instrument for paralysis and condemnation. But he never suggested abandoning the Law. He said:

Think not that I have come to abolish the law and the prophets; I have not come to abolish them but to fulfill them.

16

For truly, I say to you, till heaven and earth pass away, not an iota, not a dot, will pass from the law until all is accomplished. Whoever then relaxes one of the least of these commandments and teaches men so, shall be called least in the kingdom of heaven; but he who does them and teaches them shall be called great in the kingdom of heaven. (Matthew 5:17-19)

It is important, therefore, to study the commandments and to learn to live by them today. The coming of the Spirit of God has not cancelled them. Instead, it has put a new heart in us and has enabled us to fulfill them. If the Law was ever our enemy—and the scribes and Pharisees had made it one—it is now once again our friend. Now we can behold what a gift it is. Now we can echo the conviction of the psalmist, "I will never forget thy precepts; for by them thou hast given me life" (Psalm 119:93).

Now we are prepared to receive the following parable.

Once upon a time, a tribe of people lived between the jungle and the sea. They were very happy, for the Great Power, which is what they called their deity, had given them fertile soil for growing wheat and the jungle for gathering bananas and the sea for abundant fishing.

One day a series of disasters began to mar their idyllic existence. A young woman was walking in the field at sunset to meet her lover when an explosion suddenly rent the air, scattering her body over hundreds of yards. Some days later, a child was playing near the jungle with a sling he had fashioned from a piece of animal hide. As he reached for a nice, smooth stone for his sling, an explosion ripped through his little body as if it were made of paper. Another time, two men were pulling their nets at the mouth of the river where it joined the sea. One stepped back upon a clump of saw grass, and an explosion blew away half his body.

The council of elders met to consider the situation. They realized that their village was mined with dangerous explosives, but they didn't know what to do about it. People couldn't simply remain at home; their livelihoods and happiness depended on the freedom to move about. So they prayed to the Great Power.

"O Great Power," they said, "thou seest the calamities that have come upon us, and thou knowest how helpless we are. Do thou come speedily to our rescue and save us for thy name's sake."

Several days later, after more tragedies had occurred, a bell summoned all the people to their assembling place, and an elder stood to speak. "Last night," he said, "I had a dream. In my dream, the Great Power swept me up and revealed to me where the land mines are hidden. Here is a map of their locations. If we will learn to avoid the places marked with an X, we shall live happily ever after."

A great shout went up from the people, and they lifted the elder and carried him about on their shoulders. They made copies of the map, lest the original should ever be lost, and many of the people committed it to memory. It was, they said, the greatest gift they had ever received, and it deserved to be honored not only in their lifetime but for all generations as well.

The people who followed the map lived safely and happily ever after. But those who ignored it were destroyed, bringing sadness to the hearts of all their friends and loved ones.

The First Commandment:

No Other Gods

"You shall have no other gods before me."
(Exodus 20:3)

This is the big commandment. It has to be, for it is set at the beginning of all the commandments, and all the others depend on whether we keep this one. If we have other gods, it may not matter to us whether we steal or commit adultery or bear false witness. This one is crucial.

And we are so gullible about other gods! Or at least we used to be, when we were primitive.

There is a graphic illustration of this gullibility in the popular South African film *The Gods Must Be Crazy*. A pilot, flying over the territory of some African Bushmen, throws a a Coke bottle out of his plane. It lands near the Bushmen. They are astonished by it, for they have never seen anything like it. At first, it is a popular item in their community, for they find many uses for it. But when it becomes an object of jealousy and dissension, they wish to be rid of it, and think the gods were crazy for sending it to them.

One of the Bushmen says he will carry the bottle to the edge of the world and drop it off.

On his journey, he encounters the first white people he has ever seen and thinks they are gods. The bottle, he assumes, must belong to them, and he tries to return it. When they do not understand and refuse to accept it, he is forced to continue on his mission. Near the end of the movie, he comes to a high cliff overlooking a waterfall that fills the valley with mist. Thinking he is at the edge of the world, he casts the bottle into the mist and returns to his village.

This is the kind of mentality the Hebrew leaders were dealing with when God gave the Ten Commandments to Moses. The people were an easy prey for new gods. In their superstition, they readily accepted the existence of any gods they heard about. For a nomadic tribe constantly moving through other peoples' territories, this posed a real problem, for they were always picking up additional deities to worship. The most difficult to combat were the Baals, the agricultural deities of the Canaanites, which supposedly caused the grain to rise and the grapes to swell and the goats to become fat with kid. The blessings of these gods were tangible, and their worship often took the form of sexual relations with the sacred prostitutes at the temples of Baal. This was a very popular form of religion, and it was very hard to contravene.

You shall have no other gods before me—popular or unpopular. The meaning of the Hebrew text of this verse is a little uncertain. Some scholars translate *before* to mean "besides me," ruling out the possibility that God was willing to tolerate the existence of other gods, providing he was always first. One thing is clear, and that is the centrality God expected to enjoy in the lives of the people he had delivered from slavery and was forming in the wilderness.

Our biggest problem in dealing with the text, of course, is that we have not recently been delivered from slavery. We have not had the alien boot on our necks, forcing us to work at hard labor from dawn to dark, and received a bit of grain or gruel as our payment. We have not experienced a miraculous escape from a pursuing army and survived the hard days of adapting to a new way of life in the desert. We live in a nylon and plastic society, in which the temperature is automatically controlled and the hardest work is done by machines. The Hebrews lived in a world of pestilence and death. We live in a world of sanitation and wonder drugs. They struggled through the desert on foot. We travel in automobiles and RVs and vans and trucks, not to mention planes and helicopters and rocket ships. They existed at a time when every flame and bush seemed alive with God. We exist in an era in which faith in the supernatural is one of the least manageable of all human experiences. Were the first commandment to be framed today, said Henry Sloane Coffin, it would probably read: "Thou shalt have at least one God."

Our world has become an antiseptic against gods. It is sterile and inhospitable to them. It is like a hollow dome of human manufacture in which the only echo we hear when we try to pray is that of our own voices. Consequently, many of us have given up believing. We don't have many gods; we don't even have one.

"God used to rage at the Israelites for frequenting sacred groves," says Annie Dillard in *Teaching a Stone to Talk*. "I wish I could find one." Yet nothing is sacred any more.

A case in point is the kind of life described in Lee Iacocca's autobiography, which was on the best seller lists for months on end. He is a great American whose image has been on all our television screens, who has turned the Chrysler Motor Company around, and is rumored to be a prospective candidate for the presidency of our country. Yet there is not a single valid sign of God or of holiness in his whole life's story. His autobiography is all about ambition and promotion and getting ahead. That's what we admire today, what we hold up to our children—that crock of emptiness!

Nothing is sacred anymore. So what do we get in the place of God and the sacred groves and the great mysteries of the past? All the little gods, the demigods, of our lives.

The demigod of the home. "My home is the most important thing in my life. I will work with all my zeal to preserve it. I will sacrifice time, energy, everything, to make it a place of love and communication and satisfaction." Then one of the children goes on drugs and destroys this idyll. Or my spouse and I can't sustain our relationship, and it comes falling down like a house of cards. Or the money gets tight and we spat and all the peace and tranquility go out the window.

The demigod of the marketplace. "My business means everything to me. It hypes me up, it keeps me going. I'd rather be in there competing than doing anything else in the world. I thrive on wheeling and dealing, roaring and soaring, cutting and strutting." Then something happens to my company and I'm out on the streets, or the old ticker explodes, and they won't allow me to work more than an hour or two a day. After all, it's only a demigod, not a real god.

The demigod of leisure. "Sure, I work hard when I work, but I do it all for the sake of leisure, of getting away for a few days of golf and fishing, sailing with the kids, going down to the islands. It's my way of being good to myself." Everything for the sake of a few days off—all the overload before and after, the costs of resorts and boats and green fees, the stress of getting ready to go, the worry about things back home. This is a very small demigod.

The demigod of my own body. Without much emphasis on holiness and the Spirit, that's what life comes down to, doesn't it? My own body. So I worry about it a lot. I pamper it and starve it and feed it and exercise it and tone it and tan it and buff it and oil it and massage it and bow down to it, often in disgust, a hundred times a day. I give it too much to eat and drink, trying to make it feel good. Then I have to try to gain control again. And then I get angry when I see it all going, when I realize that my body is growing old faster than I can make it "young" again. I shout at it, "Come on! If you are the temple of the Holy Spirit, why are you collapsing this way?"

The point is that none of it amounts to very much without the Holy Spirit—not the home, not the marketplace, not our leisure, not our precious bodies. There is an emptiness in all of it when the Sacred has gone out of life. Everything begins to smell of death and decay, and at midlife especially we start to feel that life is an empty gum wrapper. The little bit of sweet has gone, and we are left with nothing now but the rotting teeth and the stench of decay.

Eugene Ionesco, the European playwright, has given us a portrait of despiritualized humanity in his play *Exit the King.* Berenger, the king, represents all of us. When the curtain rises, news is pouring into his throne room about the dismantling of the kingdom. The forests are dying, the rivers are drying up, the sun is going out, and the Milky Way is curdling. Soon, great cracks begin to appear in the walls of the castle itself, and the walls collapse.

The king grows visibly older and more and more senile. His shoulders sag, his head bends, and the crown falls and rolls away. Someone puts a nightcap on his head and brings him a hot water bottle, and he sits helpless on his throne. As his mind loses its power of retention, so that he fails to remember the people around him, they begin to disappear—poof!—one after another. Finally everyone is gone except the king and his old queen. She walks around the throne, dramatically cutting the invisible threads that still bind him to this life. Then she disappears, too. He sits alone on the throne, bathed in an eerie, gray light. Suddenly he disappears, too, and there is nothing left but the throne.

Exit the king, exit humanity, without God. It is an unforgettable picture of the emptiness, the hollowness, of life without the Holy.

You shall have no other gods before me.

The *hope*—for there must be hope—is that when we come to this point, when we have seen the barrenness of the world today without the Sacred and have seen what a poor job our demigods of home and marketplace and leisure and sensuality and all the rest do at justifying our existence and how it all comes down to the empty throne and the eerie, gray light, then we are ready to be saved. We begin to see that our history is really like that of Israel, that we, too, are in slavery and despondency and lostness, and that only a miracle of the living God will get us through the wilderness and into the Promised Land again.

No other gods—that's his condition. That's the requirement he makes. We must give up our hope in everything else and rest it all in him, letting God be God in everything, in every way. There must be no holdouts, no reservations, no hidden agendas. We must simply let him be God and listen to him for our orders. We must put him in charge of everything. We must fall down and worship him, with no other gods.

I once met a man who had been president of a bank and a leader in his community. He was also a Sunday school teacher in his church. But the Lord wasn't his God. He had a lot of other gods—a lot of demigods. He wanted a big house and a swimming pool. He wanted fancy cars for his children to drive. He wanted to be even bigger in his community. So he began embezzling funds from his bank. He took only a little at first, for it seemed a fearful thing to do. But then, when nobody noticed, he began taking more and more.

Whenever his wife asked him, "Honey, can we afford such and such?" he always said, "Yes, go ahead and get it." Then he took more money to cover the cost. "It made me feel like a big man," he said. "I was gratifying a lot of needs."

Nine years after this man began embezzling, his kingdom came apart, like Berenger's. In a period of four months, while an official investigation was being conducted, his family went from a position of luxury to near poverty. His crime was eventually reported in all the newspapers. He went to prison. His wife had to take a job. His children had to give up their cars. The family lost their home. Their whole world collapsed.

In prison, the man found his way to God. Not the God of his former life, of his flimsy respectability in the community and his Sunday school lessons, but the real God, the living God, who makes miracles and leads people through the wilderness to a Promised Land.

His whole way of looking at life and his whole way of looking at religion were changed. After that, he didn't just talk about God, he knew God. And he put God first, above everything else.

"Here's the bottom line," this man now says in talks to young people. "You will never succeed in life by trying to please yourself and fulfilling your dreams. The only way to win is by trying to please the Lord. He's the One who really counts."

No other gods. This is the most important commandment, and all the others come after it.

The Second Commandment:

No Graven Images

"You shall not make for yourself a graven image. . . ." (Exodus 20:4-6)

How do you draw God? Some artistic and inventive children have given me little drawings they have made during worship, and many of these contain representations of God. At times God looks like one of the Old Testament prophets, with a wicked eye and a great long beard. At other times, he resembles Zeus or Poseidon or another of the classical deities, with a trident or thunderbolt in his hand. Occasionally some clever child produces a drawing that simply shows a great throne with electrical currents throbbing around it, as though God were invisible and known only through his power.

Perhaps these children are familiar with the little couplet that says,

> I drew God when I was three,
> But he grew up along with me.

How do you draw God? Maybe you are too subtle, being older, to portray him with an anthropomorphic face and figure, but you see him as a God who punishes people for the bad things they do. I often encounter this in persons who have lost their jobs or are suffering from an accident. They say, "I know I have not been a very good person, and now God is getting even with me." Or you see God as a miracle worker who will answer your prayers for money or success or healing only if you can pray hard enough and in the right manner. I often see this too—people whose primary conception of God is a sort of divine filler of orders, who dispenses his blessings only after they have been requested. Perhaps you go to the other extreme and picture God the way the eighteenth-century rationalists did, as a kind of cosmic tinkerer who made the universe and set it in motion and now has very little to do with its day to day operation. This image of God must prevail for many people, or they would show more concern about how to reorder their lives before him.

How do you draw God? As traditional or contemporary? Left-wing or right-wing? Male or female? Abstract or concrete? Judgmental or merciful?

The point of the second commandment is that we shouldn't draw God at all, that we should only fall down and worship him, for God is too far beyond us to be represented by anything we might draw.

Remember the setting in which the commandments were given. God had gotten the attention of Moses by speaking to him from a bush that burned but was not consumed. When Moses wanted to know God's name in order to use it with Pharaoh, God gave only the word *Yahweh*, which means "I am who I am," nothing else. The people of Israel crowded up against the holy mountain, trying to get a glimpse of this strange deity who had commanded their escape into the desert, but they were warned that they would die if they ever saw him. Moses pleaded for a special viewing. After all, he was on the spot as the middle man. So God told him to hide himself in the cleft of a rock. Then God passed by, so that Moses saw, as the Bible quaintly puts it, only God's back parts.

The other gods were easy enough to see. They were images of men or bulls or lions or eagles. But Yahweh, the real God, was transcendent. No one could see Yahweh or take his measure. He was beyond all human understanding.

> For my thoughts are not your
>   thoughts,
>   neither are your ways my ways,
>   says the Lord.
> For as the heavens are higher than
>   the earth
>   so are my ways higher than your
>   ways
>   and my thoughts than your
>   thoughts.
>
> (Isaiah 55:8-9)

Other gods were reducible to wood and stone and metal, but not Yahweh. Other gods could be depicted in paintings and tattoos and embroidery, but not Yahweh. Other gods could be expressed in formulas and creeds and philosophies, but not Yahweh. Yahweh was the God of all gods. Nothing any human being could do would form a net to catch him. He was simply beyond all human imagining and understanding. He remained shrouded in mystery. He was, in fact, as Rudolf Otto would name him in our own day, the *Mysterium tremendum*, the most unfathomable mystery of all.

What it all comes down to, in their day and ours, is that we cannot own God.

If you think about it, there are two kinds of sin: the sin of ignoring God as though he did not exist and the sin of thinking that we possess God and have some special right to his powers and benefits. The first is the sin of secular culture and the second is the sin of religious culture. We are warned away from the first sin, ignoring God, by the first commandment, "You shall have no other gods before me." We are warned away from the second, thinking we possess God, by the second commandment, "You shall not make for yourself a graven image."

But religious people have a way of thinking that God belongs to them. We think of him in certain ways and act out our dealings with him in certain rituals, and before we can say *Constantinople*, we assume that we know all about him and what he wants and how he behaves. We may not make actual graven images of God, but we do reduce him in our minds to images that are just as small and limited. Do you remember J. B. Phillips' little book

Your God Is Too Small? That's what we do to God—we make him too small.

I have a friend whom I have known for many years. We hunt and fish together. We play cards together with our wives. We have a meal together every Saturday night. We talk about our children and share stories about what is happening to them. You might say that he is my *intimate* friend. I know all there is to know about him. Then one day, quite by accident, I discovered that my friend once worked for the CIA and that he has killed several persons, most of them by garroting—strangling them with piano wire. He has never talked to me about this, and doesn't want to talk about it now.

How do I feel? My friend isn't as completely "known" to me as I thought. There is a part of his life I have never seen. He transcends our relationship. He has other relationships that I know nothing about. He is my friend, but he is also more than my friend.

Do you suppose it's that way with God, that God is my friend but God has other business, too, that he transcends our relationship? If I know this, I will have more respect for God. I will not presume upon our acquaintance. I will not sin against him by thinking I own him or I know all there is to know about him.

God would not really be God if we were able to know everything about him. It is necessary for him to transcend our relationship, to extend far beyond the scope of his dealings with us. He is "the God beyond God," to use Paul Tillich's phrase—the God beyond everything we know about him or experience with him.

Can we talk about the scandal of the Christian faith, that this "God beyond God," unknowable, unthinkable, *Mysterium tremendum*, has made himself known in Jesus Christ, that the faceless God who showed Moses only his back parts has now revealed his face in the Man from Galilee? "He is the image of the invisible God," says the Apostle (Col. 1:15). He is the image we were told we shouldn't have.

How do we square it? We can't, say the enemies of Jesus. This is why they called Jesus a blasphemer when he identified himself with the Father in heaven. To them, it was the sheerest blasphemy for any mortal being to claim to be the image of the invisible God. God's mystery must be protected!

To me, this is what makes the Christian faith exciting. It *dares* to give a particular face to God. It dares to say, "This is what your heavenly Father is like. Anyone who has seen Jesus has seen the Father." It is like looking through a small window onto a trackless universe. God forgive us; we have seen for an instant, a moment, a microsecond, what the Father looks like, how he comports himself, how he loves us.

But let's be honest, it is only for an instant. For all we know about Jesus, there is still much we don't know. The New Testament drops its veils around him gracefully, protecting him from the open stare of the irreverent and the disinterested. The image is an icon, not an idol; it is a mere sketch, a cartoon, that invites us to gaze in God's direction but still does not fulfill our ambition to see everything, to know all about him.

More books have been written about Jesus than about any other person who ever lived. Yet the real information, the hard data on his life, are actually quite scarce. Not a single thing he ever wrote is left to us—only his sayings, sifted through several sources and finding amendment on the way. It is as though he stepped out of the fog, met a few friends, talked with them a while, and then stepped back. The fog closed around him, and the mystery of God still remains intact.

This is important, said Karl Barth, the great theologian. Jesus was like the point at the intersection of two lines, where heaven and earth came together, and a point, by definition, has no dimensions of its own; it is as if it doesn't exist. He was like a crater where a shell has exploded. The evidence that something has happened is there. But everything that produced the explosion is gone, vanished.

We must be careful not to demand too much of God's earthly image, not to become overly friendly with the deity, because he has revealed himself in a moment of love and compassion. It is easy to step across the line here and become worshipers of graven images, to reduce God to a favorite picture and then disallow the remainder of his mystery and existence.

I was reading something recently by W. E. Sangster,

the British Methodist, whom I have long admired. He was complaining about an incident at a conference. One of the conferees, a minister or an American bishop, while listening to a discussion, was idly cleaning his fingernails with the end of a small metal cross on his watch chain. Sangster said nothing at the time, but he was outraged that the man had no more respect than that for the sacredness of the cross.

But what was the cross of Jesus, really? A crude bit of wood, a vertical and a crossbar, an instrument of death, but nothing sacred in itself. Did the apostle Paul really "glory" in it, as we like to think, or did he not really glory in the fact that Yahweh, the unspeakable God, had revealed his love in Christ, who died on a cross for the sins of the world?

Dare we make an idol of the cross? Or of the Bible? Or of the little we know of Jesus himself?

There was once a woman who fell in love with a travel poster. It was a dramatic photograph showing the whitewashed buildings and Byzantine domes of the Greek island of Santorini, with the shining blue sea behind them. She asked the travel agent for a copy of the poster, and she took it home and put it up in her breakfast nook, where she would see it every morning. Soon she began to dream of going to the Greek islands and seeing this fabled view for herself.

Each time she received a paycheck, she put away a few dollars toward the realization of her dream. Eventually the day came when she flew off to Athens on the first leg of her journey. Because her tour included several days in the city of Athens, she dutifully made the rounds of the sights, but she confessed to one lady that she was not very much interested in what she was seeing, for she had really come for only one purpose: to see the beautiful scene in Santorini that was captured on her travel poster.

When the tour group left Athens, it traveled by steamer to the ancient island of Mykonos, with its twisting, narrow streets, its unforgettable harbor, its picturesque windmills, and its whitewashed buildings and Byzantine domes. Most of the people in the group oohed and ahhed at the glorious sights, and some even began to write poetry the evening they stood on the hill and watched the sun set like a fiery red wafer into the mauve and golden sea. But the woman was unyielding; she had come to see the houses and domes of Santorini.

From Mykonos, the tour transported the group to the little island of Paros. They stayed on the leeward side of the island in a hotel overlooking a beautiful bay where the fishermen brought in their catches every evening just before dinner. In the daytime, many of the party lay indolently on the crescent beach that stretched around one end of the bay. Others swam in the luminously clear waters, marveling at the beauty of their surroundings. But the woman rarely left her hotel room. She was dreaming of her special view in Santorini.

Finally, the tour arrived at Santorini. The ship sailed into the rim of the enormous volcano on which the city is perched. It was almost dusk, and the sky over the sea looked like a great bank of embers, slowly fading into night. Many people said it was the most beautiful sight they had ever seen. But the woman rode silently up the hill to the hotel, clutching her dream of the view on the poster. "Tomorrow morning, when the sun rises," she thought to herself, "I will see it." She would have only a few hours in the city, but it would be worth it. She would stand on the parapets of the city and look down across those gorgeous housetops and domes pictured on the poster. Her heart was pounding faster than she had ever known it to pound. She didn't know if she would be able to sleep.

During the night, a great storm off the coast of southern Italy moved into the Aegean Sea, bringing cooler temperatures to the region. As the cold air met the warm sea water, thick vapors rose and spread their murky blanket over everything. When the woman awoke and rushed to her balcony to look out over the view she had longed to see, everything was shrouded in fog. She could barely see the building immediately below her hotel. Later in the day, her heart heavy with disappointment, she sailed with her group toward Crete, where they would catch a plane home. She had missed everything—all the grandeur and beauty of an entire civilization—by focusing too exclusively on a single image.

Maybe this is why we are warned away from creating an image of God—even the finest of images. We might fix our sights only on it and miss everything else!

The Third Commandment:

Not Taking God's Name in Vain

"You shall not take the name of the Lord your God in vain." (Exodus 20:7)

Rubem Alves says we can paraphrase this commandment to read: "Don't use God's name unless you mean it, unless you're really serious about it."

That catches a lot of us, doesn't it?

The casual churchgoer or synagogue member who isn't really committed to a life of faith.

The person who likes to use a little profanity now and then.

The minister or Sunday school teacher who talks blithely about the Almighty without realizing what a serious act it is.

Even the government of the United States, which stamps "In God We Trust" on its money and then places its real faith in nuclear deterrents.

Using God's name without really meaning it is a matter of bad faith, really—of pretending to a relationship we don't have.

Like a woman who cleaned house for an elderly gentleman and one day slipped two checks out of his checkbook, signed his name to them, and attempted to cash them. She was only pretending that she had a right to his name.

Or two boys who, horsing around one evening with nothing to do, called a girl and pretended to be a friend of theirs who truly liked her. They didn't mean it. They weren't serious. They only pretended to be the friend.

Or a goodlooking young woman who married an unattractive man because he was wealthy, and then began to behave unfaithfully. She took his name, professing to love him, but didn't mean it. She was only pretending.

Or a scholar in a university who wanted to strengthen the chances of his manuscript's being accepted by a publisher, so forged two supporting letters from eminent authorities in his field. He had no right to use their names. He only pretended that he did.

Do you see what this commandment is all about? It is about using God's name lightly, with no seriousness, without realizing the consequences of it.

God's name, you see, is very powerful, for it represents a very powerful God. Using the name of a friend in jest is one thing, but using the name of a powerful person, of a king or a president or even one's boss, is something else. And to misuse the name of Yahweh, the most powerful being there is—why, that is almost unthinkable!

It is true that Yahweh is not God's real name. It is only a pseudonym, a made-up name, that God gave

Moses at the burning bush when Moses insisted on having a name to take to Pharaoh. "Tell him it is Yahweh," said God, "I am who I am." That was the name Moses used for him, and it stuck. Even if it was a joke, it stuck.

And because it was the only name the Jews had for God, they treated it with great respect. At one point in their history, they were so afraid of it that they didn't use it at all. Only the high priest dared to speak it, and then only after he had been ritually purified to do so. This pseudonym was more frightening than any real name, because it named the *Mysterium tremendum*, the God beyond all finding out. And nobody played around with that name!

He was in the sixth grade. His name was Elwood. Elwood was the class rascal, the one who was always getting into trouble. The teacher's name was Mrs. Crouch, and she was out of the room a lot. One day when she was out Elwood left, saying he was going to the bathroom. When he returned, he said he had seen Mrs. Crouch in the adjoining building and that she had sent for two boys in the class, Billy and Jimmy. They were to come at once and help her carry some books back to the classroom. Mrs. Crouch came back and found the boys missing. When they returned, she was upset and demanded an explanation for their absence. They said that Elwood had sent them on a fool's errand in her name. Fire in her eyes, she turned to Elwood. "Did I give you permission to use my name?" she asked. "How dare you do that?"

She was only a sixth-grade teacher.

How dare we use God's name—or even a pseudonym?

Christina Rossetti, the poet, didn't. In fact, she could not bear to see a paper with words printed on it blown about the London streets for fear the divine name might be written on it.

But most of us are not that sensitive. Our world is no longer sensitive. The name of God has undergone an enormous devaluation in recent years. It is used more frequently and less seriously, in joking and as an epithet.

Once when I was in the hospital following an appendectomy, I shared a room with a man from the South. He was one of the most naturally funny men I have ever met. One of the stories he told was of a Pentecostal street preacher who preached every Saturday morning outside the courthouse in town.

"He would get to whoopin' and hollerin'," said my friend, "and talkin' about God-this and God-that, and pretty soon a little crowd would gather around him. Then he would always say, 'Oh, I feel the Spirit comin' on me, I feel it a-comin'!'"

Next, said my friend, the preacher would wish he had a snake to handle as proof of his spiritual power. "Oh," he would say, "when I feel the Spirit, I wisht I had a snake. I wisht I had a snake!"

One Saturday morning before he went to town, my friend went down to the barn and caught a big black snake that lived there and took it to town with him. When he got out of his truck, he wrapped the snake around his arm and held it under the bib of his overalls. He walked with it that way down to the courthouse, where a crowd had gathered to hear the street preacher.

"He had just warmed up," said my friend, "and he was a-shoutin' God-this and God-that, and pretty soon he began to talk about the Spirit comin' over him and how he wanted a snake to handle. Oh, if he could only have a snake to handle. And then I throwed that old snake right out there on the sidewalk by his feet. He jumped three feet in the air, hollered the Lord's name in vain real loud, and run off down the street like he'd been bit!"

The sheriff arrested my friend for disturbing the peace, but the people in the crowd had enjoyed it so much that they took up an offering and paid his fine.

There are two examples of the devaluation of God's name in that one story. The most obvious, of course, is the way the street preacher took the name of God in vain when he forgot himself at the sight of the snake. But he also used the name of God in vain when he preached, for the preaching had no real purchase on his life and bore no true relationship to it. Which is the worse instance of devaluation? You may be right if you say the preaching, for, in that, God's name was used to defraud people.

Walter Harrelson, in his book *The Ten Commandments and Human Rights*, says that the commandment against misusing God's name comes down hard on all the preachers today who are using God's name to intimidate the poorly educated masses and thus to maintain great financial empires. The name of God is cited a thousand times in almost every religious television program to hawk books and records and magazines—to keep the money pouring in and their empires growing.

However, says Harrelson, there is guilt at the other extreme as well.

The use of the divine name for mischief is not restricted to threats of hellfire; equally appalling, I believe, is the issuing of palliatives in the name of religion, offering soothing syrup in place of a demand for justice, or speaking "peace, peace when there is no peace," or "healing the sins of a people lightly." That is what Hosea probably saw in North Israel when he spoke of "feeding on the sins of the people." (Philadelphia: Fortress Press, 1980, p. 75)

Jesus, in his time, was irate about the cheapening of the divine name.

Not every one who says to me, "Lord, Lord," shall enter the kingdom of heaven, but he who does the will of my Father who is in heaven. On that day [the day of judgment] many will say to me, "Lord, Lord, did we not prophesy in your name, and cast out demons in your name, and do many mighty works in your name?" ["Did we not build great churches and universities and preach the gospel on cable television and heal everyone who sent a donation?"] And then will I declare to them, "I never knew you; depart from me, you evildoers." (Matthew 7:21-23)

You see? A disjunction between using the divine name and acting as if God is really the Lord, acting as if the name truly means something cheapens the name of the Lord.

And then there is a consequent cheapening of all names and statements, a devaluation of all oaths, promises, sermons, protestations, advertising— everything.

William Barclay, the biblical interpreter, says that using the divine name without meaning it has weakened the three most important religious pledges most people make: the *marriage* pledge, when we promise in God's name to love and honor our partners until we die; the *baptismal* pledge, when we promise to rear children in the nurture and admonition of the Lord; and the pledge of the *sacrament*, when we receive the bread and the cup and promise to live in a renewed relationship with the Lord. (See *The Ten Commandments for Today* [Grand Rapids: Eerdman's, 1977], p. 28.) Nothing on earth is safe from the erosion of meaning once we have failed to honor the holiest name there is.

Who can see where the erosion will end? It proceeds at such a rapid pace now, implemented by the electronic media, that one can only wonder what will be the state of human relationships twenty years from now. Will anyone's word be good? Will honesty and decency and good will continue to exist as human virtues? Will there still be religion as we have known it?

I sent a package in the mail, the name of the addressee neatly printed on a sticker. Somehow, in the mysterious ways of the United States Postal

Service, the package appeared to have undergone a series of specially designed tests. First, it looked as if it had been submerged at the bottom of a muddy pond. Then it apparently found its way onto the floor of the locker room passage of the Chicago Bears. Finally, it showed signs of having been dropped from the space shuttle onto a mountainside in the Alps. When at last it made its way back to me, it bore a large rubber stamp mark that said: "NAME OBLITERATED—RETURN TO SENDER."

Name Obliterated—Return to Sender. Isn't that what is happening to the name of God today? It is being desecrated to the point of obliteration and is consequently being withdrawn to God. God is retreating into silence and mystery, and leaving us to make it on our own. That's the curse that goes with using his name without meaning it.

Hosea, in ancient times, understood this. Listen to his prophecy:

> Hear the word of the Lord, O
>   people of Israel;
>   for the Lord has a controversy
>   with the inhabitants of the land.
> There is no faithfulness or kindness,
>   and no knowledge of God in the
>   land;
>   there is swearing, lying, killing,
>   stealing, and committing
>   adultery;
>   they break all bounds and murder
>   follows murder.
> Therefore the land mourns,

> and all who dwell in it languish,
> and also the beasts of the field,
> and the birds of the air;
> and even the fish of the sea are
> taken away.

(Hosea 4:1-3)

Even the conservationists can complain because there is no knowledge of God in the land, because his name isn't honored. When we take his name in vain, without really meaning it, everything goes awry!

What's the remedy? What will restore our sense of the divine name in modern times? Perhaps the first and most logical step is to stop using it so casually, to remember who it belongs to, and to employ it only with respect and reverence. Sometimes the sense of mystery returns to our lives when we have the sensitivity to feel it. Then we must bind ourselves in genuine obedience to the One who gives us his name. He is a God of love and grace, it is true; but even love and grace carry a measure of obligation. We cannot be his people, called by his name, without living as his people. We cannot be on-again, off-again followers. There must be faithfulness, consistency, and obedience on our parts as there is on his. Every day is Gethsemane Day, when we should be asking, "Lord, what hard thing will you have me do?"

When we live that way, listening and asking, the meaning of the divine name will live again for us. This will not be true for everybody. That's not the

47

promise. But it will be true for us, for a remnant of his people. His real people are always a remnant in this life. In the life to come, it will be different. There, everybody will honor his name, for it will be celebrated as the key to heavenly existence.

Do you remember the passage from Revelation we often use at funerals?

Then he showed me the river of the water of life, bright as crystal, flowing from the throne of God and of the Lamb through the middle of the street of the city; also, on either side of the river, the tree of life with its twelve kinds of fruit, yielding its fruit each month; and the leaves of the tree were for the healing of the nations. There shall no more be anything accursed, but the throne of God and of the Lamb shall be in it, and his servants shall worship him; they shall see his face, and *his name shall be on their foreheads.* (Revelation 22:1-4, italics added)

That's wonderful, isn't it? On *yours* and *yours* and *yours* and *mine*—because we have honored it here.

The Fourth Commandment:

Keeping the Sabbath

"Remember the Sabbath day, to keep it holy."
(Exodus 20:8)

A business executive had a recurrent dream. He was driving a funny little stock car in the Indianapolis 500. He raced his little car around the track as fast as he could go, with other cars constantly roaring past, forcing him over, getting in his way. Several times, he got crossways of the track, and other cars crashed into him, sending him around and around, out of control. Each time, he would gain control again and go speeding off around the track. Finally, he was going so fast that he couldn't make a curve, and he woke up as his car plowed into a wall, turned over, and caught fire.

"I think I've figured out what it means," he said when recounting the dream. "I've been trying to go too fast and do too much. Several times lately, I have felt myself going out of control—you know, my nerves, my temper, and all that. I've got to slow down, or I'll really crash. The trouble is, there's so much to do and so little time to do it."

Do you recognize his problem? Could you put yourself in his dream and imagine it was yours?

Being too busy is one of the biggest problems we face today—maybe the biggest.

So much to do and so little time to do it. It's like a theme song. We sing it over and over—at the beginning of the day, at the end of the day, all through the day—and we're wearing ourselves out. Even our children live in a state of perpetual tiredness.

We forget that we weren't meant to live this way, that God gave us a day of rest each week to slow down and get in touch with ourselves again. God himself, says the commandment, worked six days, and on the seventh day he rested. Are we better than God? Everything was to stop on the seventh day. Not even the beasts of the field were to work. The very land was permitted to rest. The priests did no work, for in the beginning, at least, there were no instructions that the people should use the Sabbath for worship and religious education. It was simply to be a day when all work ceased and people had a chance to be physically and psychically recreated.

There was a dramatic scene in a film about a man who designed aircraft. It was at an old-fashioned airshow, where barnstorming pilots performed amazing feats for the people watching below. One pilot, who was famous for his double and triple loops, performing very tightly so that the plane seemed momentarily to flip over in the air, had broken a strut on his plane while landing. He jumped in another plane and gunned the motor. The designer, seeing him do this, shouted and waved for him to stop. The pilot, his adrenalin flowing, ignored him and roared off into the sky.

"That plane will never stand it!" said the designer. And, true enough, as the pilot was doing a sharp loop, a wing broke off, and the plane crashed.

"How did you know?" asked someone standing near the designer.

"I built it," came the reply.

We tend to cheat about observing the seventh day, to get in all the work and activity we can. *So much to do and so little time to do it.* Don't you suppose our Creator knows what we can stand, what our frames will bear? And if a Sabbath rest was important back in ancient times, when life's pressures were simpler, don't you think it is important today?

The seventh day was given for resting.

It was also given for rejoicing.

Our traditional picture of the Sabbath is admittedly not very strong on rejoicing. Most of us who had sabbatarian parents or grandparents remember it rather grimly as a day when we were not allowed to have fun. David H. C. Read recalls from his boyhood the Sunday when he was whittling on a piece of wood. His Irish grandmother, whom he describes as "a strong-minded Methodist," asked him what he was doing. "I'm making a boat," he replied innocently.

"They must be hard up for boats," she said, "if they have to be made on the Sabbath" (See Read, *This Grace Given* [Grand Rapids: Eerdman's, 1984], p. 12).

But the original spirit of the Sabbath was one of joy and gaiety. It was a time for eating and drinking and visiting with friends and family. People were not permitted to cook on the Sabbath, but they cooked the day before and had festive meals, with laughing and singing and telling stories.

This tradition is seen in the book of Nehemiah, which recounts the story of the return of the Israelites from exile and the restoration of the Law. When the Law was first read to them on the Sabbath, the people wept. But Nehemiah the governor enjoined them: "This day is holy to the Lord your God; do not mourn or weep. . . . Go your way, eat the fat and drink sweet wine and send portions to him for whom nothing is prepared; for this day is holy to our Lord; and do not be grieved, for the joy of the Lord is your strength" (Neh. 8:9-10).

Sometime between then and the time of Jesus, of course, this idea of a day of joy got messed up by people who didn't know how to rejoice. The scribes or lawyers developed thirty-nine different "families" or categories of infractions against the Law, and Jewish scholars have since listed a total of 1,521 infractions derived from these. The category of "plowing," for example, came to include such forbidden activities as spading, digging a trench, and dragging a stick across the ground. "Reaping" included picking grapes, plucking olives off the tree, and pulling off the tops of wheat.

This is what got Jesus' disciples into trouble with

the Pharisees on a Sabbath. As they passed a wheat field, they plucked some ears of grain—reaping!—and then proceeded to rub them in their hands, which was considered to be threshing.

Jesus himself got into trouble with these watchdogs of the Law by healing a man on the Sabbath. The Law was not completely unfeeling; it permitted coming to the aid of a person judged to be dying on the Sabbath. But healing anyone who was not dying must be put off until the next day.

Jesus, in the strong, prophetic way he had of dealing with the Pharisees and their intricate web of laws, cut straight to the heart of the matter. "The sabbath was made for man," he reminded them, "not man for the sabbath" (Mark 2:27). God gave the Sabbath as a day for rest and rejoicing, not for putting all human behavior in a straitjacket!

Biblical theologian Ernst Käsemann, in his book *Jesus Means Freedom*, says that this may well have been one of the most radical statements Jesus ever made. God gave his Law as a blessing, not a curse. But some people have always had a way of turning blessings into curses.

Käsemann tells the story of a small Dutch village that was being threatened by a storm. As the sea tides inched higher and higher, eroding the dikes, people gathered in the village church to decide what must be done. They were in a quandary. It was the Lord's Day, and their faith forbade their working on the Sabbath. Yet if they didn't work, they might well lose their homes.

Finally, in the heat of the debate, a young clergyman timidly mentioned the example of Jesus. "Our Lord reminds us," he said, "that the Sabbath was made for man, not man for the Sabbath."

"Aye," retorted an old man who was very conservative, "I always did suspect that our Lord Jesus was a wee bit of a liberal!"

Jesus was, if by "liberal" we mean "free"—free to feel the spirit of God, free to enjoy the Sabbath and the world his Father had made.

I have always liked the little episode narrated by Marcus Bach in his book *The Power of Perception*, about the Sunday when his father defied his strongly conservative mother and cut church to take young Marcus fishing. It was a glorious spring day, but Marcus' joy in it was marred by thoughts of a wrathful God. As they bicycled past the cemetery, with its gruesome reminders of mortality, his pleasure in the outing seemed to ebb completely. But then, out in the country, it came back again.

A flash of secret wisdom told me I knew things that even my preacher uncle did not know, knew them because I felt them on this beautiful spring morning. God liked fishing. Jesus liked fishermen. God liked this Sunday morning world. . . . God's world was life and freedom. God's world was the open road and the farmyards and the young corn coming up in clean cultivated fields. God's world was the man-sized bike and the legs that made the wheels go round. God's world was Dad and I and Lodi's Mill. God's world included people going to church or going fishing, just as long as they really loved the Lord. ([New York: Hawthorn Books, 1945] p. 135)

Later, as the boy stood by the water of Lodi's Mill, watching the green flakes of algae covering the pond, the shimmering lily pads, the beds of watercress, the silent mill wheel, and the other fishermen standing around the bank, the scent of new-greening willows brought an old hymn ringing in his mind:

> Come, thou almighty King,
> Help us thy name to sing,
> Help us to praise!
> Father all glorious,
> O'er all victorious,
> Come, and reign over us,
> Ancient of Days!

The Sabbath is a day of resting, a day of rejoicing, a day of remembering—the three "Rs." Marcus Bach was doing all three.

The Lord's Day is not the same as the Sabbath, of course. There is a long and interesting history about their relationship. The first Christians were Jews, and they continued to observe the Sabbath while observing the day of their Lord's resurrection as well. A letter from Pliny, the governor of Bithynia, to the Roman Emperor Trajan in A.D. 111 reminds us that the Christians met very early on the Lord's Day, "before it was light," to sing hymns of praise to Christ before going to work. Then they returned in the evening, following work, to have a meal together and to celebrate the sacrament of the table.

For centuries, after Christianity became separated from Judaism, the Lord's Day was not a day of rest. Then, in the eighth century, a theologian named Alcuin insisted that, for Christians, the Lord's Day is the equivalent of the Jewish Sabbath. Ever since, with brief interruptions in the Reformation, it has been thus observed.

It is true, as the great reformers Luther and Calvin reminded us, that Christians are not bound by a legalistic system and are not compelled to rest or worship on the Lord's Day. But how can we not remember the unspeakable significance of the Lord's Day? Shouldn't every Lord's Day begin with a recollection of the women who went to the tomb to anoint Christ's body with spices and of how startled they were to find the tomb empty? Shouldn't we remember the angel, who said, "He is not here, he is risen!" Wouldn't it redeem and revitalize our lives, once a week, to remember that? Wouldn't it bring us together to worship and sing hymns to Almighty God, who created the world and is still creating it in his kingdom today?

We are free in Christ. There is no doubt about that. But our very freedom compels us to remember and to worship.

Years ago, a magazine carried the true story of a man who lived during the Great Depression. The man worked at a job that paid an inadequate salary of three or four dollars per week. His wife was ill, and much of his money had to go for medicine. He got behind on his house payments, and the bank was going to foreclose on his mortgage. He went to see about another job, one in a sawmill, that would pay seven dollars a week. It was Saturday, and the owner of the mill told him to report for work the next morning at seven.

"But tomorrow is Sunday," said the man. "I go to church on Sunday."

"We work seven days a week," said the mill owner. "Plenty of people after the job—take it or leave it."

He turned it down.

His wife died in February, and in March he moved into his son's home and let the bank possess his house.

"Through it all," said his son, who wrote the story, "Dad never lost his faith in the God of the Sabbath. He wasn't an overly pious man, and he never made us kids feel that it was wrong to have fun on the Sabbath. But he loved his Lord, and he believed in a day of rest. When we buried him six years later, my sister put into words what the rest of us were thinking: 'He really knew what life is all about.'"

Compare that with the man's dream about the racetrack. "He really knew what life is all about." It makes you think, doesn't it?

The Fifth Commandment:

Honoring Father and Mother

"Honor your father and mother, that your days may be long in the land which the Lord your God gives you." (Exodus 20:12)

A boy who is playing basketball with his friends remembers that his mother said for him to be home by five. He stops the game, walks over to his coat on the fence, and checks his watch. He is honoring his father and his mother.

A woman is making a cake, using her mother's recipe. She pauses to look at the familiar handwriting on the recipe card and smiles at the memory of the paunchy little woman it evokes. She is honoring her father and mother.

A man is flying across the country on a business trip. On the way home, he deplanes at a city in the Midwest, rents a car, and drives two hundred miles to visit his father in a nursing home. He is honoring his father and his mother.

A college student is studying for a test. Some friends drop by and urge her to go to the movies. She wants to go, but remembers how hard her folks work to send her to school and decides to stay in the room and study. She is honoring her father and mother.

A child buys a Christmas present for his parents and wraps it himself. The wrapping is inexperienced and haphazard, but he is honoring his father and his mother.

A surgeon completes a difficult operation and looks at her watch. She knows her father will be having a difficult day on the anniversary of her mother's death. She slips around the corner to a phone and calls him to tell him she is thinking about him. She is honoring her father and her mother.

A couple traveling abroad pause in a cathedral before a host of candles surrounding a statue of the Virgin Mary. They are not Roman Catholics, but they drop some coins in a box and light candles for their dead parents. They are honoring their fathers and their mothers.

It is hard to define what it means to honor your father and your mother, but we know what it is when we see it. It has to do with duty, respect, care, thoughtfulness, obedience, generosity, and all sorts of human values directed toward one's parents—and grandparents. When the Bible speaks of fathers and mothers, it usually refers to all forebears, not merely the immediate past generation. Honor *all* of those who have gone before you.

It is difficult for us to imagine the importance of this commandment for the Israelites at the time God gave it to them. They had been a nation of slaves with individual allegiance to their masters, not to other family members. They had become nomads wandering in the wilderness, with no great overarching cultural mores or traditions to guide them in their behavior to one another. They were surely confused in their attitudes and competitive with one another for food and shelter and social standing.

"Honor your father and your mother," said God, "that your days may be long in the land which the Lord your God gives you." The author of Ephesians, in the New Testament, calls this "the first commandment with a promise" (Eph. 6:2). If the Israelites would follow it, they would find structure and strength to exist as a people. They would last as a nation.

We live in a time of confusion, too. The years since World War II have been a period of disintegration for many long-valued structures and traditions. Sociologists often speak of a breakdown of the nuclear family. Movies and television programs reflect the conflict between the generations, a conflict said to signal the end of civilization as we have known it. Margaret Mead, the famous anthropologist, said that ours is the first era in history when culture is determined more by the young than by the old, when children set the standards and patterns for their parents.

Does that sound crazy? Think about it a minute. Whose clothes determine today's fashion trends? The young people's. Whose taste in cars influences Tokyo and Detroit? The young people's. Whose philosophy of sexual behavior sets the standards of conduct? The young people's. Whose rhythm decides what kind of music we listen to? The young people's.

Young people, says Mead, are the only ones quick enough to adapt to our swiftly changing world. They have grown up with new math, computers, space travel, and videos. They are more comfortable with today's world than their parents are, and the parents often turn to them for guidance and approval. How can they possibly honor father and mother, those old fuddy-duddies? Surely they must despise them for being inept and out-of-tune about everything, for not being hep to the all important youth culture.

If the Ten Commandments were to be given today, the fifth commandment would probably say, "Honor your sons and your daughters, that, while you have them, your days on earth may be peaceful."

Here, we are at the root of one of the most serious problems with the fifth commandment. How do we honor fathers and mothers whom we do not respect? Even worse, how do we honor them if they do not deserve respect? Here is a mother who is a prostitute. How can a child honor her? Here is a father who gets drunk and beats his family. How can a child honor him? Did God intend for us to honor father and mother regardless of their behavior?

The chaplain in a home for abused and wayward children once told me that he could not use the Lord's Prayer at the home. When I asked why, he explained, "There is a thirteen-year-old girl at the home who, from the age of seven, was repeatedly raped by her father. Whenever she hears the word *father* it triggers a violent reaction, and she goes into a self-destructive rage."

Could such a child ever honor her father?

How does the Bible deal with this?

Jesus himself honored his father and his mother. For years, he appears to have followed Joseph's trade. Throughout his ministry, he had a tender regard for his mother. One of his final acts, as he was dying on the cross, was to provide for her future by commanding his youngest and dearest disciple, John, to take care of her.

Once, in a verbal battle with them, Jesus accused the Pharisees of breaking the Law of God by not truly honoring their parents. "You use a mere technicality in the Law to avoid giving them money when they need it," he said. There was a practice, called *corban*, of setting aside part of one's money for God; the money was not to be used for any other purpose. But some people apparently declared any money to be corban that they didn't want to use for anything else. So, when an aged father and mother were sick and destitute for funds, a Pharisee could say, "Sorry, Dad, but you know I've dedicated my money to God and can't let you have any of it."

"You make void the law of God," said Jesus, "by resorting to this convenient tradition" (Mark 7:13, paraphrase). Jesus didn't raise the question of whether the parents were deserving. For him, the law about honoring father and mother was the Law of God, and that was enough.

Is this still not specific enough? Then let's look further, into the teachings of Jesus' followers. Often, when we cannot find what we want in Jesus' sayings, we will find it in the teachings of his followers, for they were the interpreters of his faith. He sent them forth with the authority to preach and teach and baptize in his name.

Let's look in the book of Colossians, which, if it was not written directly by the apostle Paul, was at least strongly influenced by his teaching and writing. Chapter 3 of Colossians is one of those great mountain-peak chapters, at once sonorous and majestic and filled with good advice. "If then you have been raised with Christ, seek the things that are above, where Christ is, seated at the right hand of God. Set your minds on things that are above, not on things that are on earth. For you have died, and your life is hid with Christ in God" (Colossians 3:1-3).

The stage is set. If you call yourself a Christian, then you must desire to behave in a heavenly manner. There follows one of Paul's favorite rhetorical devices, a catalogue of evil behavior we are to avoid. (It is similar to the great catalogue in Galatians 5.) "Put to death therefore what is earthly in you: fornication, impurity, passion, evil desire, and covetousness. . . . In these you once walked, when you lived in them. But now put them all away: anger, wrath, malice, slander, and foul talk from your mouth (Colossians 3:5-8). Instead, he says, as God's chosen people we are to put on "compassion, kindness, lowliness, meekness, and patience, forbearing one another and if one has a complaint against another, forgiving each other; as the Lord has forgiven you, so you also must forgive. And above all these put on love, which binds everything together in perfect harmony" (Colossians 3:5-8, 12-14).

And there's one more thing:

Wives, be subject to your husbands, as is fitting in the Lord. Husbands, love your wives, and do not be harsh with them. Children, obey your parents in everything, for this pleases the Lord. Fathers, do not provoke your children, lest they become discouraged. Slaves, obey in everything those who are your earthly masters. . . . Masters, treat your slaves justly and fairly, knowing that you also have a Master in heaven. (Colossians 3:18-22, 4:1)

Do you see how it all connects? Of course we live in confusing times. Of course children often know more than their parents. Of course parents may sometimes drive us wild. Of course the spirit of rebellion is strong. But when the way of Christ prevails in our lives, when we see what God is up to in the world, bringing it into the way of his kingdom, then the spirit of submission is stronger. Then the hidden rationality of God's Law is made visible, and we want to obey it, even at great cost to ourselves.

There is a beautiful picture of the connection in Jesus' story of the prodigal son. The son rebelled against tradition and against his father, demanding his inheritance while the father was still living. How did the father treat him? He could have refused. He might even have disinherited the boy. It was an upstart thing to do, and fathers were really supreme in those days. Roman fathers even had the power to have their sons executed, no questions asked.

But the father chose to be submissive. He chose to give in to the son despite all the cultural pressures against it. We know how his other son felt. We can imagine what his friends and neighbors must have said: "Poor old Seth, he doesn't know the first thing about handling boys."

The father gave in to save the relationship between himself and his younger son—and save it he did! When the boy got hungry, he came home, groveling. "Father," he admitted, "I have sinned against heaven and before you; I am no longer worthy to be called your son" (Luke 15:21).

What did the father do? Did he put his foot on the boy's neck and say, "Darned right, you aren't"? No, the boy was submissive, and so was the father. He took the boy in his arms and kissed him. Then he shouted to his servants, "Bring quickly the best robe, and put it on him; and put a ring on his hand, and shoes on his feet; and bring the fatted calf and kill it, and let us eat and make merry; for this my son was dead, and is alive again; he was lost, and is found" (Luke 15:22-24).

Do you see what God intended by the Law and how the Law is fulfilled in the Spirit of Christ? It was never meant to be a law of oppression, with one person lording it over another. It was meant to be a guideline for love and compassion and forgiveness, for living with one another in joy and peace. Children are always to obey their parents, for this pleases the Lord; and parents are never to provoke their children, lest the children become disheartened. Life is beautiful in the Lord, if we will only let it be that way.

The theme of mutual submission is central to one of the great novels of our time, Alan Paton's *Cry, the Beloved Country.* Like the parable of the prodigal son, Paton's story is about a boy who leaves home and gets into trouble. The boy is Absalom Kumalo, a young black man in South Africa. He is the son of a minister named Stephen Kumalo, who is pastor of a church in the small village of Ndotsheni. Absalom has gone off to Johannesburg, the big city. His letters have stopped coming for a long time, and old Stephen Kumalo goes to the city to look for him. While Stephen is there searching, Absalom enters the house of a white man to steal. Surprised in the act, he shoots the white man. The city is outraged. Absalom is tried, convicted, and sentenced to hang. There is a tearful reunion when Stephen visits him in prison. But nothing can be done, and Stephen, heavy-hearted, returns home to Ndotsheni. The grief he carries in his bosom is hard, palpable, like a stone that throbs. "There are times, no doubt," says Paton, "when God seems no more to be about the world."

Stephen visits the father of the man who was shot to express his sorrow and regret. The man, whose name is Jarvis, is a wealthy landowner. He has been reading the manuscript of a book his son was writing, in which the son speaks of the way the black race has been exploited in South Africa. It has affected his heart, and he forgives Stephen's son for the shooting. He resolves, moreover, to help the people of Stephen Kumalo's village. He sends giant bulldozers to erect a dam to provide water.

The people of Ndotsheni are full of excitement. Soon the fields will be green again, and they can have cattle. There will be milk for the children to drink. Their sons and daughters will no longer go off to the city to live, for there will be life in the village.

On the fourteenth day of the month, before his son is to die on the fifteenth, Stephen Kumalo takes a bottle of tea and some cakes made of maize and walks up into the mountain called Emoyeni, which means "in the winds." It stands high above Carisbrooke and the tops of the other mountains. He has gone up twice before in his life, once when Absalom was a boy and was deathly ill and another time when a white man offered him a job in a store, which made him think of leaving the ministry. When he reaches the top, panting and tired, he sits and looks across the valley, remembering the first time he came there and how much he loves the boy who is about to die. Having recovered from his climb, he sets about his prayers. First, he confesses all his sins. Then he prays prayers of thanksgiving for all the good people in his life, and for Jarvis, the white man who is reviving the village. At some point, he falls asleep, for he is weary from the climb.

Awaking with a start, he thinks of his son. If only he had found him sooner, perhaps he could have saved him. But then the village would have no dam, no water. He wonders if his son is sleeping, and prays that he is. Then he himself falls asleep again. When he wakes, there is a faint light in the east, and he feels a sense of panic. But it is only four o'clock.

He stands, numb from the cold and from sleeping on the rock. He watches the light gradually coming into the eastern sky as he takes out the tea and maize cakes and sets them on a stone. He gives thanks, eats the cakes, and drinks the tea. Then he gives himself to earnest prayer, looking eastward after each petition. The sky lightens and lightens, until he knows it is almost time. Then he rises to his feet. He takes off his hat, lays it on the ground, and stands with his hands clasped before him. As he waits, the sun rises in the east.

What has Paton tried to say? His story is a picture of the fifth commandment. If the boy had only honored his father and his mother, he would not have gotten into trouble; he would not have died. It is also a picture of New Testament faith. The father loves the child, loves him almost beyond bearing. The white man, who has so much property, shares it with the black people who have nothing. And the hope of the kingdom, like the dam at Ndotsheni and new life for the village, is that the kingdom is coming, it is on its way, for God, who loves us and submits himself to us, will redeem everything.

The Sixth Commandment:

Not Killing

"You shall not kill." (Exodus 20:13)

Truman Capote's *In Cold Blood* is the gripping real-life story of two former convicts, Richard Hickock and Perry Smith, who brutally murdered an entire family in the community of Holcomb, Kansas. These men had appeared sane enough; Perry had even painted a large, pastel portrait of Christ and presented it to the chaplain at the prison. But when they got out on parole, they planned their gruesome escapade with the intensity of madmen.

"We're gonna go in there," said one of them, "and splatter those walls with hair."

They did not know the victims, people named Clutter. But they had heard that Mr. Clutter often kept large sums of cash in his home. They expected to use the money to finance a trip to Mexico. As it turned out, there was no money. But they left the Clutters dead—tied-up and shotgunned—all over the house.

This is the sort of amoral act the sixth commandment is aimed at. Some translations, such as the New English Bible, read for it, "You shall not commit murder." It was not intended to stop all killing. The Jewish people themselves were to take the lives of those who broke certain of the commandments. And they obviously continued to believe in waging "just" and "holy" wars. But the wanton and indiscriminate killing of an individual by another individual had to stop. An orderly society simply could not tolerate private acts of violence.

We have to bear in mind, of course, the sort of people who first received the commandments. They were not a Sunday school class on an afternoon's outing. They were a wild and uncontrollable tribe of former slaves. Many were probably thugs and cutthroats. Moses himself, their leader, had once murdered a man in Egypt. Without the Law to guide them, they would probably have destroyed their whole civilization by fighting among themselves.

This is not to say that we are much better than they were. Henry Sloane Coffin, the distinguished president of Union Theological Seminary in New York, once preached a sermon on the sixth commandment to a sophisticated congregation in one of the finer churches of that city. He began by noting the element of humor in preaching on such a topic to such a respectable group of people. Surely none of them was a murderer. But then, said Dr. Coffin, there are ways of killing that do not always connect us with the crime. Tenement owners may neglect the installation of proper wiring in their buildings. Manufacturers may fail to observe certain safety precautions for their employees. Contractors may erect substandard bridges. The point the commandment makes, said Dr. Coffin, is that human life is sacred, made in the image of God, and we must treat it so.

Human life is sacred because it is made in the image of God. The rationale was there even before the commandment. In the book of Genesis, Noah and his sons were given a warning after the great flood: "Whoever sheds the blood of man, by man shall his blood be shed; for God made man in his own image" (Genesis 9:6). The blood was thought to be the seat of the spirit. As the spirit of human beings was fashioned in the Spirit of God, spilling another's blood was an act of desecration, or attacking God himself.

What the commandment calls for, then, is a reverence for all life. Life belongs to God, and we can never take it casually or with impunity.

This has insurmountable implications for four of the most important issues facing us today.

The first issue is *abortion*. It is not a simple issue. Undoubtedly, there are times when a pregnant woman ought, for physical or psychological reasons, to have an abortion, regardless of the stage of fetal development. And the question of when a fetus becomes a person with human rights is highly debatable. Both the highest medical and religious authorities differ on the subject. But whenever a decision is made to have an abortion, it must be made under full awareness of the sixth commandment, that it is always wrong to take a life. If one wrong must be committed in order to avoid another wrong, then so be it. Sometimes that's the choice we have to make. But life is always sacred to God.

The second issue is *euthanasia,* or mercy killing. Suppose a child is hopelessly deformed at birth, so that it will require constant care for a lifetime. Wouldn't it be merciful to everyone involved if the child were allowed to die? A young person sustains an injury in an accident and lingers for years in a coma. Isn't this a case in which the Hippocratic oath ought to be set aside and the person permitted to go? An old person is dying of cancer. It is a slow, painful death, with disfigurement and humiliation. Wouldn't it be the gracious thing for a fatal dose of medication to be left on the patient's bedside table, allowing her to depart with choice and dignity? Yet we are never free of the commandment. It is God's eternal safeguard against our assuming the power of deciding whether other people should live or die.

The third issue is *capital punishment.* It was not an issue for the Jews, although they did not use it as freely as we might think. The Mishnah, or collection of oral interpretations of the Law, indicates that they were so careful about the rights of an accused person that they almost never put anyone to death. But the intervening centuries, and the additional opportunity they have given us to ponder the commandment, have led many thoughtful persons to believe that, if we truly have a reverence for all life, we cannot possibly decide arbitrarily to take the life of anyone, even a killer like Richard Hickock or Perry Smith.

William Barclay, in his commentary on the commandments, says that the love ethic of the Christian spirit can never wish anything for a criminal but the criminal's conversion and reformation and that this can never be accomplished by capital punishment. "You shall not kill"—once we have accepted it as our biblical mandate—is difficult to obey in one instance and disregard in another.

The fourth issue is *suicide*, which has been a matter of growing concern in recent years. As life becomes increasingly complicated and stressful in modern society, more and more people are driven to consider life termination as a means of escaping the spiraling pressures. Some kind of identity crisis is often present in a suicide—the person does not know who he or she is, feels unworthy in the eyes of others, or simply has not had a positive enough experience of life to reinforce the desire to live. But, while potential victims of suicide may not be deterred by religious considerations, if they are either Jewish or Christian they can hardly avoid the personal message being flashed to them by the sixth commandment: "You shall not kill." Life is created by God and belongs to God. It is not ours to destroy.

Did I say there are four issues today that stand under the judgment of this commandment? There are five. We cannot avoid the largest, most complicated issue of all, which is *war*. Wars appear to be inevitable in the history of humankind. The Jews of the Old Testament times were never troubled by thoughts of the moral indefensibility of waging war on other tribes or nations. Occasionally they even recorded their feelings that God was displeased because they had been too soft on their enemies and allowed them to live. But sensibilities shaped by centuries of living with the commandment "You shall not kill" are bound to see things differently. Who can say that Barclay is not right to be horrified at memories of the bombing of Dresden, an unarmed, neutral city, by the Allies at the end of World War II, an incendiary bombing which resulted in the deaths of perhaps a quarter of a million people, and of the dropping of the first atomic bomb on Hiroshima, which took the lives of 71,000 people, almost all of whom were civilians? Who is not scandalized and horrified at the reminder that the nuclear powers, the United States and the Soviet Union, now hold in the superarsenals the equivalent of over a trillion tons of TNT, or more than thirty tons for every man, woman, and child living on the face of the planet? Or that there is enough nerve gas in existence today to destroy all life in an area of 500,000,000 square miles, which is more than eight times the total area of our world? "You shall not kill"—and we have turned the whole world into a gigantic time bomb!

These are all controversial matters—abortion, euthanasia, capital punishment, suicide, war—and they are not easily resolved. But Coffin had a good thought about getting a handle on them. He remembered the word of the New Testament writer: "Whatever you do, in word or deed, do everything in the name of the Lord Jesus" (Col. 3:17). What we cannot do in Jesus' name, we are not to do at all. If we cannot abort a fetus in Jesus' name, then we shouldn't do it. If we cannot end a patient's life in Jesus' name, then we shouldn't do it. If we cannot take the life of a criminal in Jesus' name, then we shouldn't do it. If we cannot take our own lives in Jesus' name, then we shouldn't do it. If we cannot build superarsenals or go to war in Jesus' name, then we shouldn't do it. "Do everything in the name of the Lord Jesus."

Jesus, you see, brought us an interpretation of the Law that was higher than anyone had ever understood.

You have heard that it was said to the men of old, "You shall not kill; and whoever kills shall be liable to judgment." But I say to you that every one who is angry with his brother shall be liable to judgment; whoever insults his brother shall be liable to the council, and whoever says, "You fool!" shall be liable to the hell of fire. (Matthew 5:21-22)

Killing isn't merely a matter of what we do. It is a matter of what we think and say; it is a matter of *attitude*. If I hate someone, if I am angry with someone, then I have the spirit of death in my heart, the very spirit that produces killing. In the kingdom of God, this is opposed to God's will. It is an infraction of the Law of the Spirit. What I say to you, said

Jesus, is that you must "love your enemies and pray for those who persecute you, so that you may be sons of your Father who is in heaven"—for God loves all his children, even our enemies, and "makes his sun rise on the evil and on the good, and sends rain on the just and on the unjust" (Matthew 5:44-45).

In other words, we are to do more than refrain from killing. We are to be so converted to a spirit of love that we want to give life, not take it. Christians are to be a life-giving people. We are to be channels of grace for a life-giving God. Not only are we not to take away life, we are actually to bestow life.

This is the whole point of the cross, isn't it? People hated Jesus so much that they wanted to kill him. But Jesus didn't hate them back. Instead, he submitted to their hate and derision; he let them take his life. And, at the very time when they were taking his life and spitting on him, he was forgiving them and holding out life to them. The murderer dying on the cross by him understood. "Jesus," he said, "remember me when you come into your kingdom." And Jesus said to him, "Truly, I say to you, today you will be with me in Paradise" (Luke 23:42-43).

Life, not death.

Giving it, not taking it.

This is what it's all about. This is what the Christian learns as his or her heart is converted and comes into full understanding.

It's what Elisabeth Elliot learned in the jungles of South America. Elisabeth and her husband, Jim, were young missionaries to the Auca Indians of Ecuador. The Aucas were an extremely primitive tribe in the interior country along the Curaray River. Leaving their wives behind, Jim and four other young men flew into the Auca territory, dropping gifts and a message in Auca language that said, "We like you." They landed on a strip of sand by the river and waited for the Indians to come. Their diaries revealed their excitement at the hope of bringing Christ to the Aucas. But Jim and the other men never returned. When a search party flew over the beach, they saw that the little plane had been stripped of its covering, and they spotted a body floating in the water. A ground party later found four more bodies. They had all been killed by lances. One lance was even wrapped in a paper bearing the message the men had dropped.

Elisabeth and the other wives returned to the States to see their families. Elisabeth took with her a baby named Valerie, who had been born to her and Jim only a few months previously.

In churches all over the world, prayers ascended for the wives and families of the slain missionaries. But the wives themselves were praying for the Aucas. We look forward, they said, to the day when the Aucas will join us in Christian praise.

Less than three years after the death of her husband, Elisabeth was sitting in a leaf-thatched hut only a few miles from the beach where Jim was killed. In another leaf house ten feet away sat two of the seven men who had murdered the missionaries.

One of the men had just helped little Valerie, now three-and-a-half, roast a plantain.

Was it a miracle? Perhaps. The wives had returned to Ecuador. They had studied the Aucan language and prayed for an opportunity to work with the Indians. A new missionary pilot continued to fly over the Auca territory and drop gifts, proclaiming the missionaries' friendship. At last, three Auca women came in from the jungle and said that the tribe was willing for the missionary wives to live among them. The men said that they had killed the missionaries out of fear; they thought they might have been cannibals. The women went and took the gospel to those who had been savages. They taught them the commandments, including the one that says, "You shall not kill." But they also taught them the love of Christ, which goes beyond both killing and hating, and which is building the new world of the Spirit.

Coffin was right, wasn't he? If we can't do something in the name of Jesus, then we shouldn't do it at all.

The Seventh Commandment:

Not Committing Adultery

"You shall not commit adultery." (Exodus 20:14)

Probably nothing, except death itself, causes more pain in the human community than adultery. There once was a family in which the father and mother were attractive and outgoing, and the children were bright, inquisitive, and well-liked. The father contracted a mysterious disease of the muscles and nearly died. It left him drawn and incapacitated. His wife, beautiful and high-spirited, began to be seen with other men. She had affair after affair and became the talk of the town. One man who was in love with her embezzled funds to buy her presents and was sent to prison. Her children grew up in an aura of shame and whispers. The oldest son, quick-witted and intelligent, threw himself into schoolwork and graduated from the university with honors. He won a high-paying job on the West Coast and quickly moved up in the company. Eventually, though, he took his own life because he could not resolve the deep feelings of hurt and confusion he continued to experience.

It is almost always the same. Even when adultery

does not result in divorce, it leaves ineradicable scars on people's memories and relationships. The problem is a breach of faith. The physical act of betrayal signals an important psychological message. It says, "I no longer truly value our relationship. My own desires are more important than love." Like killing, which is prohibited by the commandment before this one, and stealing, which is prohibited because it is an act of taking what does not belong to one, adultery is a violation of rights, and almost everybody is hurt by it.

Oh, we are great rationalizers, of course, and will take comfort in the fact that adultery is so commonplace today. This is the age of *Dallas* and *Knot's Landing* and all the soap operas that hold millions enthralled by their continuous game of musical beds. It is the era of X-rated movies and X-rated newsstands, when Hollywood is convinced it must show frontal nudity and bedroom scenes in order to entice fourteen-year-olds into the theater. It isn't any wonder that adultery doesn't raise many eyebrows these days—it has become as common as breakfast cereal and the morning paper.

It is an interesting fact that adultery was also extremely common among the peoples surrounding the ancient Israelites. For many of them, sex was a great, creative mystery, linking them with the gods who created the world and gave reproductive powers to their grain and cattle. Therefore, the people even worshiped in a sexual manner, engaging in physical relationships in their temples and holy places. In many ancient cultures, women were required to serve as temple prostitutes before they could marry and have families of their own.

But God, who blessed the Israelites with a set of commandments that would enable them to become a nation of unusual influence in the history of the world, forbade them to engage in sexual liaisons outside of marriage. They were to live above the lust and desire that ruled other people—and for good reason.

There is a story to the effect that God discussed the Ten Commandments with the angels before he gave the commandments to the Jews. Some of the angels thought the seventh commandment, "You shall not commit adultery," was too stringent and ought to be deleted.

"What do you mean, too stringent?" asked God.

"Well," said one of the angels, "it's unnatural. Human beings may be only a little lower than we, but they are also only a little higher than the beasts of the field, and no such restrictions are placed on the beasts of the field. They roam about and have sex with other animals as they please. Why should men and women be more restricted than they?"

"Because," said God, "men and women were created for meaningful relationships with one another and with me. They were made for love. There was no point in making them if they were to live with no more self-discipline than the beasts. If they cannot learn to be faithful to one another in a small thing like sexuality, how will they ever learn to be faithful to me?"

Faithfulness is the key. God made us to be faithful to one another and to be faithful to him, and when we are unfaithful to one another, to our families, we are also unfaithful to him.

The book of Hosea, one of Israel's great contributions to world literature, is an unforgettable picture of how faithfulness is a whole and cannot be divided. The people of Israel had fallen into widespread adultery, worshiping in the fanes and temples of agricultural deities and indulging in all kinds of sexual excesses. So God tells his prophet Hosea to take as a sign of his nation's unfaithfulness a wife who is a harlot. "Go, take to yourself a wife of harlotry and have children of harlotry, for the land commits great harlotry by forsaking the Lord" (Hosea 1:2).

The book tells of Hosea's terrible suffering because his wife sexually betrays him, and at the same time, eloquently portrays the unhappiness of God when his people turn their backs on him to seek their own pleasures.

The result of such infidelity, says the book, is destruction of those who engage in it.

> Nettles shall possess their precious
> things of silver;
> thorns shall be in their tents.

(Hosea 9:6)

Families and nations cannot be strong where there is a betrayal of trust.

83

Is it necessary to paint the despair of those who "trust in the flesh," as the Bible puts it, and neglect their covenants of relationship? Look at the Times Square area of New York City, the largest concentration of pornographic bookstores, movies, and flesh shows in the world, where prostitutes approach their customers as freely as if they were Girl Scouts selling cookies. It is the nearest thing to hell on earth one is likely to see, perhaps worse than anything Dante imagined in his *Inferno.* Many of the people there, once feverishly driven by sexual urges, are poor, burned-out human beings for whom sex is only a ghoulish residue, a devalued form of bartering in which they long ago lost their most precious possessions.

Sexual urges. Desires. They're the problem, aren't they? We have strong desires, and, being weak, think we must gratify them. This is why Jesus identified the desires themselves with committing adultery. He reminded his followers: "You have heard that it was said, 'You shall not commit adultery.' But I say to you that every one who looks at a woman lustfully has already committed adultery with her in his heart" (Matthew 5:27-28).

That seems awfully hard, but there's more.

If your right eye causes you to sin, pluck it out and throw it away; it is better that you lose one of your members than that your whole body be thrown into hell. And if your right hand causes you to sin, cut it off and throw it away; it is better that you lose one of your members than that your whole body go into hell. (Matthew 5:29-30)

And here is something else Jesus said: "Whoever divorces his wife and marries another, commits adultery against her; and if she divorces her husband and marries another, she commits adultery" (Mark 10:11-12).

Did Jesus really expect his followers to be able to live by such strict interpretations of the Law? Did he expect *us* to live by them? How can we avoid having desires? Even President Carter, the "born again" president, admitted that he had had lust in his heart. And what of all those who are divorced and remarried? Are they living in open adultery?

The point is the same one Jesus made about the commandment against killing when he said that killing always begins as an act of hate in one's heart and that anyone who is angry with someone else is liable to the judgment. The issues of life spring from the heart. We do what we believe and feel. If therefore we would control what we do, we must first gain a measure of control over what we believe and feel. It is not the body that is guilty of adultery, it is the heart. If our hearts are converted to God and God's Spirit, we shall be safe from temptation.

One of the most powerful statements ever made about the heart and sexuality, not barring even Augustine's *Confessions*, is "The War Within: An Anatomy of Lust," an article that appeared in the fall 1982 issue of *Leadership* magazine. This article, written by a Christian minister whose name was withheld, tells in graphic terms the story of the minister's own battle with lust. At first, he said, he was attracted by the foldouts in pornographic magazines and other nude photographs of beautiful women. Then, one night when he was attending a meeting in Rochester, New York, a picture of an exotic dancer in a Rochester guidebook led him to a bar where the dancer was performing a striptease. He afterwards swore he would not go to such a place again. But his desire had grown so strong that he couldn't resist. Lust, he discovered, always points forward. Once it has taken hold of you, you cannot go back to a former level of desire.

Although filled with self-loathing, the man began slipping into pornographic movies and reading X-rated magazines. On a trip to Washington, D.C., he went to a bar that featured nude dancing and found himself pulling out money, with other customers, and stuffing it into the garter of a girl who danced only a few inches away from him. Staggering out of the bar, he had the feeling that he could never return to innocence. He wanted to go home and tell his wife. But when he got there, he couldn't do it. He didn't have the courage.

The minister promised himself that he would never again enter such an establishment, that he would break the hold of sexual desire on his life. He was frightened because he saw himself becoming schizophrenic. He let God into most of the areas of his life but not into the sexual area. That one he reserved for himself. He thought he could lick the problem of lust by himself, if indeed he really wanted to lick it. Sometimes he wasn't sure he wanted to.

One day he flew to Boston, where he was to lead a spiritual-life conference in New Hampshire. He was elated about the trip, because he loved the New England coastline. But, during the night he spent in Boston, he found himself wandering about the seedy area of the city, looking for porno shows. Soon he was in an establishment where the customers sat behind a ring of shuttered windows to watch nude women dancing on a wooden platform. He put a coin in a slot, and the shutters opened for three minutes. Then the shutters closed. He put another coin in and watched another three minutes. He said he dropped in quarters "like a frantic long-distance caller at a pay phone."

Waves of guilt washed over him again that night, as they so often had before. He hoped that the trip up the coast the next day would expunge the feelings and restore his sense of joy before he arrived at the conference. But it didn't. For the first time in his life, he did not enjoy his drive through New England. His mind kept reverting to the cheap thrill he had felt watching that revolving platform with the nude women on it. He couldn't feel pleasure in anything. He wondered if he was going crazy.

At the conference, he made his contribution limply and routinely. People applauded as if it were meaningful to them. He went to his room at night and pondered what was happening to him.

Three days later, he was having coffee with an old friend who was pastor of one of the largest churches in the South. Never before had he divulged to anyone the details of his lust life. But now he felt that he must tell someone or lose his mind. He began confessing his problem to the friend. Suddenly the friend began to weep. The weeping became convulsive. At last, the pastor admitted he was not weeping for his friend, but for himself. He, too, had had a terrible problem with lust. In fact, his problem was much worse. He had indulged his desires much more than the first minister. He reached in his pocket and pulled out a prescription. It was for the drugs he took daily to combat a venereal disease. The man's life was in shambles. He and his wife were at that very moment engaged in divorce proceedings.

This shook the man more than ever. Was his own life on an inexorable path to ruin, like his friend's? Would the lust that had seized control of his heart continue to twist and distort his emotions until it destroyed him?

While these sobering questions haunted his mind, he began reading a little book by François Mauriac called *What I Believe*. In the book, the great French novelist talks about purity of heart. Human sexuality, he explains, has extraordinary power in our lives. The only thing that can control it is the sense of purity. But what will give us purity? Mauriac ticks off the futile things people do to try to regain purity. Then he quotes the Sermon on the Mount: "Blessed are the pure in heart, for they shall see God" (Matthew 5:8).

Only the desire to see God, says Mauriac, will bring us to purity. Nothing else will do it.

The minister was stunned. He thought he had tried all the arguments against lust, but here was one he had missed. He had not wanted to see God. Suddenly, he realized what he had been missing, what his lust was robbing him of: intimacy with God. He began to pray. He poured out his heart to God. He asked for forgiveness. And, after all those years, he said, God was there for him. After a long separation, they were together again. The healing had begun.

He told his wife. As painful as it was, she tried to understand, to forgive him.

The war wasn't over. He had made an important step, but continued to be tempted. Once he yielded again, in the North Beach section of San Francisco, and went into another twenty-five-cent peep show. But not ten seconds passed, he said, before he felt himself gripped by horror and ran out of the place. He didn't quit running until he was out of the North Beach area. Then he prayed for strength and walked away.

Now, he says, he is relatively free of the compulsion. He can pause before a newsstand and not pick up an X-rated magazine. He can pass a porno theater without wanting to go in. In his heart, there is a sense of joy and peace, of mystical union with God.

His wife feels it, too. They are enjoying their sexual life together as never before. He begins to understand, he says, why the biblical writers often employed the experience of sexual intimacy as a metaphor for spiritual ecstasy. When we know God, everything in our lives is enriched.

Do you see why Christ said that lust is the equivalent of adultery, and that anyone whose eye offends him should pluck out the eye rather than have his whole body cast into torment? He was not being hard; he was being realistic. Lust and adultery have to do with self-will, with the gratification of impulses that are merely physical. Peace and joy come by doing God's will. When God rules in our hearts, when he alone is supreme, we will have no trouble with temptation. When the soul is filled with him, it has no room for adulterous thoughts.

The Eighth Commandment:
Not Stealing

"You shall not steal." (Exodus 20:15)

Stealing is universal. There is no one who, at some time in his or her life, has not been guilty of it. When the word *stealing* is mentioned, our thoughts usually fly to dramatic instances of stealing—bank robberies, train robberies, major embezzlement, car theft, breaking and entering, stock fraud, or, in these technological times, computer theft and record piracy. But there are many small kinds of theft as well—the store manager who overcharges customers; the salesman who pads expense accounts; the housewife who shoplifts in the grocery store; the student who copies someone else's homework; the employee who places personal phone calls on the office account; the person who cheats on an IRS return.

Ministers have been known to steal sermons from other ministers. Robert Moats Miller, in his biography of Harry Emerson Fosdick, tells about the time Fosdick slipped into a little church in Maine and heard the young minister preach one of his sermons. Afterwards, at the door, Fosdick told the minister what a good sermon he thought it was and asked how long it took to prepare it. "About three hours," said the young cleric.

"You're a fast worker," said Fosdick. "It took me twenty-one hours!"

But Fosdick was not hard on the young man, for he remembered occasions when he had been sorely tempted to use someone else's material. In fact, Dr. Miller observes in the biography that Fosdick did often use quotations from secondary sources he had read without giving credit to the author who had done the spadework!

The point is that there is a blurred line between some forms of stealing and not stealing, and most of us either live in the blur or get lost in it from time to time. Even if we are not outright thieves, the kind who will ever go to prison, we are adept at stealing time, ideas, reputation, attention, honors, all sorts of things.

And it is important to remember that we never steal anything without paying for it. Although no policeman ever knocks at our doors and no prison bars ever close behind us and our photographs are never in the papers or on television, we still pay for what we have done. We pay in terms of our character, our innocence, our sense of inner trust, and our spiritual purity.

Dean Madison Sarratt of Vanderbilt University taught freshman math for many years. Former students remember his saying, "Today I am going to give you two examinations, one in trigonometry and one in honesty. I hope you will pass both of them. But if you must fail one, let it be trigonometry. There are many good men in the world today who cannot pass an examination in trigonometry, but there are no good men who cannot pass an examination in honesty."

What makes us steal? Psychiatrist Eric Thiburn says there are three primary reasons. The first is that some people are simply amoral; they cannot tell the difference between right and wrong. Small children usually fall in this category, as well as some adults with a defective moral aptitude. The second reason is that some of us cannot restrain our impulses when presented with the opportunity to take what is not ours. "It seems so easy. Nobody will know if I take this." The third reason is that some of us think we are avenging injustice by stealing. Maybe we were poor as youngsters, and it is our way of getting even. Maybe, like Robin Hood, we rob the rich to give to the poor. Or maybe we simply want to hurt the rich, who have more than they deserve.

But the result of widespread stealing, whatever its reasons, is an uneasy society. When property is not safe, life itself is restless. Then people must always be on guard against losing their possessions. We become a civilization of locks and bolts and security systems.

People who do not live in metropolitan areas must wonder about the effect on persons who live under the constant threat of assault or theft. A man and his wife were staying in a hotel in New York. The man was anxious to get started for the day, so he left his wife behind to do her hair and went to have breakfast. As he walked down the street, someone bumped him in the crowd. He reached for his breast pocket and felt that his wallet was missing. Turning, he saw the man who bumped him hurrying toward a subway. Being a large man and unafraid, he gave chase, caught the man, threw him up against a wall, and reached in his pockets to retrieve the stolen wallet. He didn't know what to do with the man. He had heard that pressing charges required a lot of time, and he had only a short time left to be in the city. So he shook him vigorously and turned him loose. By this time, he was so upset that he didn't feel like eating breakfast, so he retracted his steps back to his hotel.

"I haven't had breakfast," he said to his wife as he entered the room.

"I know," his wife said. "You left your wallet in the room."

Mortified, the man looked in the wallet he had taken and located the stranger's business address. He went to the address and sheepishly apologized for his terrible mistake.

"That's all right," said the generous victim, accepting his wallet. "I've been mugged so many times in this city I wasn't about to offer any resistance!"

God gave the Jews a commandment against stealing so their society would not be one of fear and uncertainty.

But, theologically, there was a deeper reason for

the commandment. It had to do with God's idea of property, that there should be enough for everybody in the world and nobody would need to take anyone else's. It is true, as some have contended, that God didn't create everyone equal to everyone else. It is inevitable, in a world like ours, that some people will end up with more possessions than others. This happens even when we play a friendly game of Monopoly. But God gave us enough resources so that no person should ever want for what is necessary for life. Food, shelter, clothing, and fuel, said Thoreau, these are the basics for survival; and there are enough of each, if we are sensitive to God's plan of stewardship, for every person in the world.

God even gave the Jews the concept of the jubilee year. Every fiftieth year, property was to revert to its original ownership, so that people who had lost everything through bad management or theft or for any other reason would be restored to their homes.

There is no evidence that the jubilee concept ever worked. On the contrary, the Jews became as greedy as any other people, and we have terrible stories like the one about Ahab and Jezebel, who had a man named Naboth put to death so they could take his vineyard (I Kings 21), and the one told by Nathan to David about the rich man with many flocks who stole his poor neighbor's lamb to feed a visitor (II Samuel 12). And Jesus told a story about a wealthy man who was clothed in purple and linens and dined sumptuously every day while a poor, sick beggar lay at his gate (Luke 16).

This is where the Christian ethic comes in. People did not live by the commandments. There was lying and stealing and killing. So God sent his only begotten Son with the promise of a kingdom where "neither moth nor rust consumes and where thieves do not break in and steal" (Matthew 6:20), where there would be neither rich nor poor, getting nor taking, needing nor denying. In the meantime, those who walked in the way of Christ were to love one another so much that all stealing would be abolished.

In the book of Luke, we are given a picture of the effect of Christ on a man's life. The man was a minor official in the government, but he had the power to levy taxes on the people of his region and to keep all the money over a certain amount specified by the government. He had obviously done very well on this formula and lived in a large house. Then one day he met the Master, and his life was completely changed. He no longer needed to feel important by living in a big house with many servants. He said, "Behold, Lord, the half of my goods I give to the poor; and if I have defrauded any one of anything, I restore it fourfold" (Luke 19:8).

This is the Christian way. When we enter a relationship with Christ, we no longer need what we thought we needed. We no longer feel a right to take what is not ours to take. We no longer worry that others have more than we. We see that everything belongs to God, and we are his servants, ready to do his will. We become givers and not takers!

The Christian is to live in the light, not in the darkness. "Let the thief no longer steal," said Paul, "but rather let him labor, doing honest work with his hands, so that he may be able to give to those in need" (Ephesians 4:28). You see, we are to be givers, not takers. We are to "walk in love, as Christ loved us and gave himself up for us, a fragrant offering and sacrifice to God" (Ephesians 5:2).

Those who continue to steal after they have met Christ are still living in darkness. The worst the disciples could say about Judas after he had led the soldiers to the Lord and betrayed him with a kiss was that he was a thief—he kept their treasury and stole from it! To them, this was a sign that Judas belonged to the darkness and not to the light. If we are truly converted, if our hearts belong to God in Christ, we shall want to give, not take, and bless the world, not curse it.

Two women worked for an advertising agency. (We'll call them Betty and Jane.) When calls from potential clients came into the agency switchboard, they were routinely posted in boxes on the agents' doors. One day, Betty was passing Jane's office and noticed a call slip in her box. Jane was not in. Betty thought for a few minutes, then walked past Jane's box and took the slip. She called the client, arranged a meeting, and made a sale. Over a period of six or seven months, she did this several times. It was as easy as eating a piece of cake. Betty picked up several thousand dollars in extra commissions, and nobody was the wiser—she thought.

Then one day Jane stepped into Betty's office and asked, "Are you doing anything tonight?"

"No," said Betty, "why do you ask?"

"I'm supposed to see someone about a new radio account," said Jane, "and I can't make it. I have a meeting at church. I thought maybe you'd take the appointment for me."

Betty was happy to take the appointment and the commission that went with it. What could be easier?

Jane approached her with a similar request two weeks later. This time she said she had two luncheon appointments on the same day, and gave one to Betty. Betty took it and made a sale. But she also began to wonder.

One morning Betty came into Jane's office. She looked as if she hadn't slept well the night before and was very distraught.

"I need to talk to you," she said. "You've been throwing clients my way. Why?"

Jane smiled sweetly at her. "I had more than I needed," she said, "more than I could really take care of."

"You know, don't you?" asked Betty.

"Know what?"

"That I took some of your calls."

"You must have needed them," said Jane. "Yes, I have been giving you some of my clients. I thought there must be a reason, that you really needed the money."

Betty was silent for a moment. Tears welled up in

her eyes. "I never thought of it as being particularly wrong," she said, "until now. Now I see how terrible it is." A big tear pulled loose and fled down her cheek. "It's the nicest thing anybody ever did for me," she said, "and I feel so ashamed."

I wish I knew the rest of the story. I like to think that Betty's life was changed, that she saw in Jane a model of Christian love that helped to reshape her values, that enabled her to live in the light as Jane lived in the light.

At any rate, this is what the commandment is about. We are not to steal, because stealing has no part in the ministry of love God has given to his people.

The Ninth Commandment:

Not Speaking Falsely of One's Neighbor

"You shall not bear false witness against your neighbor." (Exodus 20:16)

A high school student is walking down the hall and speaks to a friend. The friend turns her head and passes without speaking. Puzzled, the student asks another friend, "What's wrong with Donna? She snubbed me in the hall."

"Oh," says the friend, "she's probably heard what Betty is saying about you, that you made a pass at Donna's boyfriend."

"But I didn't!" says the student.

"I know, but that's what Betty is telling."

A young executive is up for promotion. When he doesn't get it, he asks his supervisor why.

"Well, it's hard to say," says the supervisor. "But I expect that the rumors about your drinking problem didn't help you."

"Drinking problem!" says the man. "But I don't have a drinking problem!"

The supervisor studies the young man's face a moment and shrugs his shoulders. "It's always hard to tell about rumors," he says. "Maybe somebody started this one to keep you from getting the job."

A woman who has been a housewife for several

years wants to return to her work as a teacher. She applies for a position with a private institution and is turned down. Querying a friend on the school board, she learns that someone on the board reported that she once had a nervous breakdown and might prove unstable in the classroom.

"But I never had a nervous breakdown," she says. "I once went into the hospital for a checkup and some rest, but it wasn't a nervous breakdown."

"I'm sorry," says her friend, "but you know how conservative a school board can be."

The mischief and damage done in the human community by false statements! It is no wonder that the little book of James compares the tongue to a torch that is carried into a drought-parched forest, where it ignites fires that quickly rage out of control and spread destruction that can never be repaired (James 3:5)! And it is no wonder that God gave the commandment "You shall not bear false witness against your neighbor."

The commandment was probably intended originally as a check against false accusations in a court of law. For many years, Israel was governed by patriarchs and judges, and the system of local courts was very important. We noted when talking about the commandment against killing how careful the Hebrews were to protect the rights of accused persons. The ninth commandment was another link in the armor of justice. Divine judgment would fall upon the person who gave false testimony against another person in a trial.

But, as most biblical scholars note, the commandment needs to be seen in the context of the Bible's attitude toward lying as a whole. The devil is "a liar," said Jesus, "and the father of lies" (John 8:44). The serpent in the garden of Eden lied to Eve about the fruit God told her and Adam not to eat (Genesis 3:4-5). David lied when he sent Uriah into the heat of the battle so he could take Uriah's wife, Bathsheba (II Samuel 11:6-17). The prophets constantly derided colleagues who did not speak the truth (Isaiah 9:13, Jeremiah 29:1, Zechariah 13:3). The opponents of Stephen, the Christian preacher, went secretly to others and accused him of uttering blasphemy against Moses and God, and thus brought about his death (Acts 6:11-12). Lying, gossip, and false reports were among the most execrable sins a person could commit.

Unfortunately, the business of bearing false witness has not died out with the passing of time. On the contrary, it seems to be as healthy as ever, despite the commandment and all the other biblical teachings.

A few months ago, when I was preaching in another city, a woman came to me with tears in her eyes. She was so agitated that she tore the strap off her purse as she talked. A friend had been telling tales on her—outrageous tales—and she didn't know what to do about it. "Have you tried talking to your friend?" I asked her.

"Yes," she said, "but she denies it."

I asked if she thought the friend might be telling

what she thought was the truth because other persons were lying to her.

"No," she said. "I'd like to believe that, but I can't. Several persons have reported her conversations with them, and they all heard the same things. She's making it all up and then lying about it to me."

"Why do you think she's doing it?" I asked.

"Because my daughter got into a certain school, and hers didn't," she said. "She turned funny when our daughters got their notifications, and now she's trying to get even with me."

I had a letter from a man whose wife had left him. To be certain that she got custody of their only child, she began a slander campaign against him. She told mutual friends that he had made sexual advances toward the child. Soon the word had spread through the small community in which they lived. It affected the man's professional status in the community. People he worked with began to treat him warily, suspiciously. His job and health were endangered.

In Keith Miller's book *The Dream*, Miller imagines that God whisks him up one night and takes him on a quick tour of Christendom. As they are flying through the clouds, they suddenly dive toward the lights of the city below. As they approach, Miller can make out the steeple of a church. There are lights in one wing of the building where a meeting is taking place. Suddenly they are in the room at the meeting, hearing everything that transpires.

A big, red-faced man in an expensive business suit is standing up and almost shouting at someone across the room.

"I don't care if he has done a good job for ten years, the secretary claimed he tried to talk her into having sex with him!"

"Wow!" says Miller.

"Shhh!" says God. "Listen."

A mild-mannered man across the room tries to respond. "But he *denies* it!" says the man.

"Listen," replies the big man. "We just announced a three-million-dollar building fund campaign last weekend. If it gets out that we're tolerating sin among the staff, our new building won't have an ice cube's chance in hell—if you'll pardon the reference, Reverend," he says, turning to the nervous-looking man at the end of the table.

Someone else remembers what happened in a church in a nearby town when it was discovered that the minister had cheated on his income tax and the board had let him stay: giving by the membership took an immediate nosedive!

The big man, feeling that everyone is with him now, comes to the point. He wants to offer the employee in question a compromise solution: if he will quietly resign and leave, they will help him find another job. If he doesn't, they will threaten to see that he never works in a church again.

No one says anything. Finally, the meek-mannered man asks the minister what he thinks.

The room is hushed.

The minister takes off his glasses and looks at the ceiling a moment as he chews on the left earpiece.

What he says, in essence, is: "As you know, Bill and I are good friends. I think he's done a fine job for us, and I would certainly like to stand by him. But it's true there have been some rumors. And this new sanctuary is something I've been praying for for a long time. I would hate to see it jeopardized. So, for the sake of the church—and for Bill's own good—I guess I have to agree with the chairman. We ought to help him find another place."

Miller is about to say something when he feels himself being propelled into the night air again.

"Did you hear that?" says God.

Miller is quiet a moment. Then he says: "Well, You have to admit You've made it pretty clear that both adultery and fornication are serious offenses."

"But he *didn't do it!*" shouts God. "Don't you see, they're supposed to be that man's brothers. But he's not even in the meeting. They didn't call him in to talk it over with him or give him a chance. That secretary of his is so sexually hung up she thinks *everybody* is in love with her. Because he was kind and friendly to her, she developed a fantasy that he was interested in her sexually, and when she found out she was wrong, her pride was so hurt that she accused him. Unfortunately, this isn't the first time this has happened in My church." (*The Dream* [Waco, Tex.: Word Books, 1985], pp. 15-17.)

The devil is the father of lies.

We have to remember that Christ himself was

brought to trial and then executed on a similar pastiche of lies and fabrications. Here he was, the Word of God in the flesh, "full of grace and truth" (John 1:14). John, the writer of the Gospel, loved this irony. "The law was given by Moses," he said; "grace and truth came through Jesus Christ" (John 1:17). "I am the light of the world," John has Jesus say (John 8:12), and "I am the way, the truth, and the life" (John 14:6). Yet the workers of evil, by telling lies, managed to bring "the way, the truth, and the life" into the dock and by false accusations to have him crucified!

Pilate, the Roman governor, was caught in the middle. The Jewish leaders, because they could not bestow the death penalty, wanted him to try the case. "What has he done?" Pilate asked them.

"Never mind," they said. "If he weren't a terrible fellow we wouldn't be bringing him to you."

"That's not enough to hold him on," said Pilate. "You'll have to tell me more."

So they accused Jesus of being a seditionist and plotting to overthrow the government. "He says he is the King of the Jews," they said.

"Are you the King of the Jews?" Pilate asked Jesus when they were alone in his council chambers.

"Do you say this of your own accord," asked Jesus, "or did others say it to you about me?"

You see? "Do you know it for a fact, or is it gossip?" Jesus was supposed to be on trial, but it was the evil tongues of the Jewish leaders that were really on trial!

"My kingship is not of this world," Jesus said.

"Then you really are a king?" asked Pilate.

"You say that I am a king," said Jesus. "For this I was born, and for this I came into the world, to bear witness to the truth. Every one who is of the truth hears my voice."

And Pilate, poor Pilate, caught in a reverie, or perhaps merely echoing his inner confusion, asked, "What is truth?" (John 18:28-38)

What is truth? This is the philosopher's question. Pilate should have asked, "*Who* is truth?" For the Lord of all truth was standing before him, the Lord whose kingdom is poised against all evil and all falsehood and all lying and all gossip. If Pilate had only been of a different bent, more of a questing nature, he might have fallen on his knees and been saved that day. But he didn't understand. He let truth be crucified, and went down in the history of infamy as one of the saddest figures of all times.

Oh, he had the last word, to be sure. He made a plaque for the soldiers to nail on Jesus's cross, with the inscription, "Jesus of Nazareth, the King of the Jews." They had come with the accusation, branding him with treason, and Pilate had decided that Jesus really was a king. But Pilate didn't have the courage to defend the truth. He was like a lot of people who stand by while others are crucified; he wasn't about to risk anything personal to stop a crime.

God, on the other hand, who *had* risked something personal, raised the crucified Jesus from death. He made truth triumphant after all. He identified truth with eternity, with that which will live, and identified falsehood with death and hell, that which will perish. In the book of Revelation, at the very end of the Bible, the visionary John sees an angel take hold of the devil, "that ancient serpent," and bind him for a thousand years, so "that he should deceive the nations no more" (Revelation 20:1-3).

And Christians, by this immortal act, are given encouragement always to side with Christ and the truth, and never to use their tongues to speak evil of others. Now that we are in Christ, says Paul, we are to put off the old nature that is "corrupt through deceitful lusts" and put on the nature of Christ himself. "Therefore," he says, "putting away falsehood, let every one speak the truth with his neighbor, for we are members one of another" (Ephesians 4:25). Our new relationship of love and community is to prevail over every temptation to speak falsely about other persons. If we do speak falsely, then we are still walking in darkness, and there is real question about whether we are truly in Christ.

A few years ago, an attorney from a Northwestern state decided to run for the city council in his community. He was feeling stale in his profession and thought this would give him new vitality. Soon his cleverness of speech and delight in talking began to carry him away, and he realized he was making irresponsible statements about his opponent. But he was careful. He never made these statements to reporters or in places where they would go on the record. He simply planted them in the minds of friends at the country club or over cocktails at a party.

The stories soon circulated, as gossip will. Then the attorney spread them further by asking "Say, do you think it's true what I've been hearing about so-and-so?" The week before the election, he appeared to be leading his opponent by at least ten points.

Three days before the election, the attorney's wife had a heart attack and was placed in intensive care, hovering between life and death. He spent almost ten hours in the ICU waiting room.

During those ten hours, which were marked mostly by solitude and apprehension, he had a chance to realize what was happening to him. His life had become so caught up in lies and innuendoes that he was like Pilate; he no longer knew what the truth was. Somehow his existence seemed shoddy and unbecoming in the light of his wife's condition. He felt a desperate sense of emptiness and self-betrayal. How had he allowed it to happen? What could he do?

There in the waiting room, he cried—not outer tears but inner tears, deep in his heart—and asked God to forgive him. A sense of peace came over him. When the doctor finally told him that his wife was stable and apparently out of danger, he went into her room and held her hand and kissed her. This time he cried tears of outward joy.

It was nine in the morning. He had not been to

bed all night, and his face was stubbled with whiskers. But instead of going home, he went to his opponent's office and confessed what he had done.

"It was like a sickness," he said, "a disease I couldn't shake, once it had infected me. I am going to bow out of the race."

And he did. He went on local television news that evening and told people that he was resigning in favor of his opponent, who was a fine, Christian man. "I have heard some ugly rumors about him," he said, "but they are untrue. I know, because I started most of them myself. I am ashamed of what I have done, and I want you all to know it. God has forgiven me. I hope you can, too."

The attorney's wife recovered, and they are still living happily in their community. He regarded his experience as a religious event in his life, and it drew him closer to his church. Today he teaches a young adults' class in the church school. And every once in a while, he says, he gives the class a lesson on truthfulness and honesty.

"It is a part of being in Christ," he says, " and it is important to all of us."

The Tenth Commandment:
Not Coveting

"You shall not covet your neighbor's wife, or his manservant, or his maidservant, or his ox, or his ass, or anything that is your neighbor's." (Exodus 20:17)

Anthropologically, this commandment is an interesting picture of Jewish life after the Israelites became an established nation. It projects the average home as a sort of mini-plantation, with a nuclear family, male and female servants, and beasts of burden—which suggests that this commandment, or at least the present form of it, did not belong to the wilderness period but to the later existence of Israel.

Theologically, this commandment is the opposite of the first one, "You shall have no other gods before me." If we love God with all our hearts and minds and souls, as the first commandment interpreted to mean, our desires will not stray and we will not trifle with our neighbors' possessions.

Psychologically, it is one of the most impossible of the commandments to keep, for we are always prone to envy the situations or possessions of those around us.

The human spirit has always been covetous. Adam and Eve desired the fruit from the one tree that was forbidden to them in the garden of Eden.

Cain wanted Abel's easy way with God. Jacob coveted his brother Esau's birthright. Ahab craved Naboth's vineyard. David desired Uriah's wife. James and John wanted first place in the kingdom of God.

I remember hearing D. T. Niles, the great evangelist from Sri Lanka, telling about his sons and how carefully they watched to see that one did not get more than the other. The family had banana trees in the back garden of their home, and each morning Mrs. Niles placed bananas by the children's plates. Each morning, as faithfully as clockwork, the boys measured their bananas to see who had received the longer or shorter one.

Jealousy and covetousness are endemic in the human situation. A popular cartoon shows an aerial view of the corners of four pastures at the point where they intersect. There is a cow in each pasture, and each cow is reaching through the fence to eat the grass in the next pasture! We smile, not because of what this cartoon says about cows, but because of what it says about us. The grass on the other side of the fence always appears a little greener to us, too.

A teacher in a laboratory school in Great Britain tried an experiment. She gave each of ten children in a classroom a different toy, left them alone, and videotaped their behavior for the next fifteen minutes from a hidden observation point. Within sixty seconds, two of the children were pulling at others' toys, while a third child greedily collected the toys those two had laid aside. At the end of the quarter-hour, three children were in possession of two toys each; three had none; two had different toys from the ones with which they had begun; and two were huddled in corners, clutching the toys they had been given and warily eyeing the other children.

Mere *children* covet one another's possessions. Yet God has the audacity to say, "Don't covet your neighbor's house or wife or anything belonging to your neighbor"! What hope do any of us have of keeping such a commandment?

Even the apostle Paul, who called himself "a Pharisee of the Pharisees," admitted he could not keep it. "I should not have known what it is to covet," he said, "if the law had not said, 'You shall not covet'" (Romans 7:7). But knowing he wasn't supposed to do it seemed to work against him. "The very commandment which promised life proved to be death to me" (Romans 7:10).

Paul doesn't tell us exactly what he coveted; we are left to our conjectures. Perhaps it was some noble position among the Romans that led to his zealous persecution of the early Christians. Perhaps it was wealth and a great house constructed of marble, with a gracious atrium and private baths and servants caring for everything. Perhaps it was recognition as a writer and a scholar. (Those who have never worked in a university or graduate school are probably unaware of the feverish jealousy with which some scholars regard one another's work.) There is even a hint, after Paul became a Christian, of his great ambition, of the inner drive that led him to become the first and foremost of the exegetes of the faith in those early years.

Paul says "Sin used the law to kill me, to slay me." Coveting—craving what belonged to others—was his undoing.

Who is immune to it? The human spirit, especially in its more imaginative and energetic forms, is restless, overleaping, driving, ambitious, zealous for improvement.

And why not? Isn't our situation improved by such a spirit? If people didn't covet better things, would we have seen the advances made in medicine and technology and transportation? Would we have had television and computers and skyscrapers? Would we have had the great novels and paintings and plays?

That is the other side—the rationalization—that it is coveting, craving, the desire for something better, that leads to all the improvements in the human condition. Bernard de Mandeville, an English philosopher in the eighteenth century, flatly asserted that sin makes the world go around. There would be no commerce, no education, no roads or cities, he said, were it not for people's greed and ambition.

This is a hard argument to counter.

But Jesus spoke of the pathos in our situation that leads us to want what we do not need and, in reaching to get it, to miss the most important things in our lives.

Do you remember his story of a rich man, a farmer, who had such a bumper crop one year that he planned to pull down his old barns and build big, new superbarns to hold everything? What had made him greedy and ambitious? Had he coveted the wealth and power of a neighbor during his own lean years? Was he trying to prove himself to someone—his wife, his children, his own father, perhaps? At any rate, it was a tragedy. "Soul," he said to himself, "you have a great deal laid up for years to come. You can eat and drink and be merry."

A British clergyman, reading this passage, commented, "What a pity, that he mistook his stomach for his soul!"

And that very night the man died, leaving it all behind—everything his covetous heart had desired.

That's the pity, you see. Most of the things we covet enlarge our stomachs or our spleens or our bank accounts or our real estate holdings or our influence in the community—*but not our souls.* The very things we covet *diminish* our souls.

There was once a boy who grew up in a poor house in the valley. The house had no indoor plumbing and was heated only by a large fireplace in the kitchen. The roof was made of tin and often had to be repaired to stop the leaks.

On the hill above the valley stood a magnificent house made of stone. Those who had visited the house said it was the most modern home they had ever seen, with every convenience a person could wish. It was beautiful on the hilltop, and the boy never tired of looking at it. Often in the evening, when his chores were done and he had eaten his supper, he would sit on the rough little porch of his family's small house and stare up at the mansion above, dreaming of a day when he would become rich and buy it for himself.

Fired by this ambition from an early age, the boy studied hard and did well in school. He went off to college and passed all his courses with flying colors. Then he came back to town, borrowed some money to buy a small business, and worked energetically until he was able to buy another business and then another. Finally, when the people who lived in the great house had all passed away and an heir was willing to sell the property, he bought it and moved into it with his growing family. The desire of a lifetime had been realized, and everyone in the little community talked about how the boy from the valley who had always wanted to move into the great house on the hill had finally achieved his dream. The story was often told by parents wishing to instill ambition in their children.

As the years went by, however, the man found that he was not exactly happy in his new life on the top of the hill. His children were lazy and ungrateful and did poorly in school. His parents, who never moved out of the old house in the valley, eventually died, and their house fell into worse repair than ever. His hair turning white and his body developing more and more ways of dysfunctioning, the man looked down on the old house and remembered the excitement of his youthful dreams. Why wasn't he happier, he wondered, now that he was such a success?

One day the man's youngest daughter got married. There was a big wedding at the church and a festive reception at the home on the hilltop. When it was over and the man's daughter had driven off in a car with her new husband, the man wandered out to the edge of the yard in his tuxedo and sat with a cigarette in his hand, blowing smoke rings and looking down the hill to the decaying shack where he had grown up.

Musing about life and its ironies, he had an insight that he had never had before. The view from the old homestead where he grew up was much finer than the view he now possessed. From the front porch of the little house in the valley, he could always look up to the big house on the hill and admire its beauty and magnificence. But once he possessed the big house, he no longer saw and admired it. Now his view was of the little house in the valley. He had traded a grander view for a lesser one.

A person's life, said Jesus, doesn't consist in the abundance of his or her possessions. It has a lot more to do with a viewpoint, a place to stand and admire the world, a sense of God's love and presence in our lives.

John Macy, in the play *The Morning After the Miracle*, tells Helen Keller and Anne Sullivan that the book they are writing together will make them rich. Helen puts her arms around John and Anne and says, "We *are* rich. We have each other."

You see the difference? This is what the commandments really meant us to see, that if we love God and put him first in our lives we shall not hunger for what we do not have. We shall not make ourselves anxious and fretful by yearning for what someone else has that we don't.

This is why some people adopt vows of poverty, chastity, and obedience. They don't do it to flagellate themselves, to punish themselves for some enormous wrongdoing. They do it to give the love of God a larger place in their lives, to give it a better chance to survive and flourish in their personalties. And some of these people are the happiest people in the world. Homeless, penniless, submissive to the will of other persons, they are rich. They know the truth of John Cage's statement that "Everything we do is music, and everywhere is the best seat."

The human spirit was not made to be satisfied by things. It was made to be satisfied by fellowship with God. And only God can fill the void in our lives that we try to fill with desire and ambition.

There was a Jewish woman who grew up over the small store her father owned on the lower West Side of New York City. When she went to college, she met and later married the son of a prosperous Jewish family in a Southern city. They acquired a beautiful home and began raising a family of their own. Over the years, the woman developed an insatiable appetite for possessions—clothes, cars, jewelry—and frequently went on shopping expeditions that cost thousands of dollars. She drove her husband to expand his business, to earn more and more money, to redecorate and refurnish their lovely house, and to have lavish parties her friends would remember and talk about. Always she justified what she was doing by saying, "I was very poor when I was young, and I cannot help wanting things now." If her husband complained, she said, "You have always had beautiful things; now it is my turn."

One night the couple's two beautiful daughters were killed in an automobile collision on their way home from a party. The fiancé of one of the daughters was also killed.

The woman cried for weeks. Nothing would console her. She decided that she and her husband must move to another house, that they must get away from the memories of their children. They bought an expensive place in another neighborhood and had it entirely redecorated. As long as the woman was supervising the redecoration, she seemed reasonably happy. But as soon as it was finished, she began to cry all the time again and missed the first house, where the children had grown up.

She had a nervous breakdown and went to an expensive clinic for several months.

When she returned home, barely holding onto life, she wanted to see her father, who still lived in New York. Her husband put her on a plane. On the Sabbath, her father asked her to go to synagogue with him. She refused. She hadn't been to synagogue in years. The next week, he asked again. This time she went with him.

Something happened to her as she listened to the rabbi chanting the old prayers. "It was like the voice of an angel speaking in the desert of my life," she said.

In college, she had studied to become a nurse. Now, she went home and enrolled in a nursing course. When she had finished it, she took a job in a local hospital. Eighteen months later, she received recognition from the hospital administration as one of the most selfless and devoted nurses on their staff. Her whole life was turned around, transformed.

What she had discovered, what she had heard in the ancient tones of the Hebrew prayers in her father's synagogue, was the secret at the heart of the commandments and the Christian gospel: Life is in God, not in things. When God is at the center, when he has preeminence over everything, we are happy regardless of our homes or our bank accounts or our titles or anything else.

"A man is never so truly and intensely himself," said W. R. Inge, the famous Dean of St. Paul's, "as when he is most possessed by God."

Appendix 1

Jesus and the Commandments

"Think not that I have come to abolish the law and the prophets; I have come not to abolish them but to fulfil them. For truly, I say to you, till heaven and earth pass away, not an iota, not a dot, will pass from the law until all is accomplished. Whoever then relaxes one of the least of these commandments and teaches men so, shall be called least in the kingdom of heaven; but he who does them and teaches them shall be called great in the kingdom of heaven. For I tell you, unless your righteousness exceeds that of the scribes and Pharisees, you will never enter the kingdom of heaven." (Matthew 5:17-20)

"The Lord God Almighty gave the commandments to the Jews," screamed the television preacher, "and then he sent Jesus. He sent Jesus and repealed the Law. He repealed the Law because people couldn't live by it, and he gave us grace."

The preacher's theology couldn't have been more wrong. The Law was a gift of God, just as the

Messiah was. Jesus himself said that he did not come to abolish the Law, but to fulfill or complete it.

How did Jesus fulfill the commandments? He did it in three ways:

(1) by the example of his life;
(2) by his teachings to the disciples, the crowds, and the scribes and Pharisees;
(3) by his Messiahship of obedience and death, which ushered in a new kingdom of the Spirit.

In all these ways, which will presently receive a fuller commentary, Jesus stood against the false understanding of the commandments that dominated Hebrew religion in his time. Repeatedly, he confronted this understanding with the original intention of God in giving the commandments, that they were to be a guide to gracious and holy living, not a cruel instrument for manipulating society along certain prescribed routes of behavior.

There is a clear picture of the confrontation in Mark 10:1-52, which contains the following accounts.

(1) *Verses 2-12*: The Pharisees test Jesus on the subject of divorce.
(2) *Verses 13-16*: Jesus receives little children and declares that the kingdom is for such as they.
(3) *Verses 17-31*: Jesus tells a rich ruler who has scrupulously observed the commandments that he yet lacks something.
(4) *Verses 32-34*: Jesus predicts his death in Jerusalem.
(5) *Verses 35-45*: James and John ask for places of honor in

the kingdom, but Jesus says that whoever would be great must be a servant.

(6) *Verses 46-52*: A blind man named Bartimaeus "sees" what others have missed, that Jesus is the Messiah, and receives his sight.

It is almost as if Mark were purposely sketching a synopsis of the various elements of Jesus' confrontation with the Jews' mistaken understanding of the nature of the commandments. The picture is so complete that it bears further study:

(1) *Verses 2-12*. The Pharisees regarded the Law as a matter of mere legality. Because Moses had said that a man might divorce his wife for the most insubstantial reasons, they admitted divorce with ease and frequency. By their method of interpretation, a man could obtain a divorce on the ground of his wife's being habitually unpleasant or a poor cook.

Far from abrogating the Law, Jesus upheld it in its strictest interpretation. His theology of marriage reached back to the initial creation itself. God created male and female, and marriage cements the two as if they had become a single flesh. Since God himself has united two persons in marriage, no flimsy legal interpretation can clear the way for their separation. Jesus was not opposed to the original commandment but to the unjustifiable and often silly additions devised through the years by the lawyers!

(2) *Verses 13-16*. By contrast with the scribes and Pharisees, little children are the real models for

living in God's kingdom. Their hearts are innocent and untouched by guile.

(3) *Verses 17-31.* The rich ruler comes to Jesus as the exceptional Pharisee. He is one who has attended to the Law all his life and yet also has a good heart. He admires Jesus and wishes to become one of his disciples. But Jesus points out the insufficiency of a mere legal approach to the Law. The man has doubtless tithed all his life; yet he has accumulated far more of the world's goods than other people, and these impair his ability to be a completely devoted follower. "Go, sell what you have, and give to the poor," says Jesus, "and come, follow me" (v. 21). The man cannot do it. His spirit is too weak and poor to go beyond the legal limits. His merely keeping the Law, as punctiliously as he has done it, has not prepared him for a true understanding of God's intentions.

(4) *Verses 32-34.* Jesus sees clearly where his confrontation with the Pharisees and lawyers is leading: he will die for having clashed with them. But they will not have the last word. God's power is at work in him and will vindicate his understanding!

(5) *Verses 35-45.* When James and John ask for special recognition in the kingdom, they are unwittingly imitating the character of the scribes and Pharisees, who love places of honor among their fellows. Jesus reminds them that the spirit of God's kingdom is radically different; it is a spirit of love and servitude.

(6) *Verses 46-52.* A blind man, one of the uneducated people of the countryside and thus a stark contrast to the highly educated scribes and Pharisees, recognizes despite his condition that Jesus is the Messiah, the Son of David, sent from God, and calls to him out of his physical darkness. It is God's way of dramatizing the corruptness and failure of the legal system in Jesus' day and the necessity to go beyond it with a new spirit.

Because of the insufficiency of human wisdom and the unreliability of the human heart, evil had triumphed over good in the world. The very commandments God had given as an aid to human behavior had been turned to wicked purposes and were used as instruments of a totalitarian mind set. The Messiah was sent into the world to break the power of this twisted situation and free people for a new understanding of God *and* the commandments.

I. Jesus' Example

As we said, Jesus countered the Pharisees' understanding of the commandments by his *example.* He lived as one who understood the real intention of the commandments and would not be bamboozled or intimidated by all the amendments to them manufactured by the lawyers.

The Gospel of Mark sets the accounts of Jesus' confrontation with the Pharisees over the Law very near the opening of his ministry, signalling the cruciality of his theology of the commandments for everything that happened in his ministry. The shadow of the confrontation is, in fact, the shadow of the cross, for it leads eventually to his death. Paul would rightly understand, when he wrote his letter to the Romans, that the battle over the Law was the central issue of Jesus' life and crucifixion.

Jesus consorted freely with persons who were not rigid observers of the Law, as the Pharisees were. He called as one of his disciples a man named Levi, the son of Alphaeus, who was a tax-collector. Tax-collectors necessarily handled foreign currencies, some of which proclaimed the lordship of Caesar. They were on this account deemed singular violators of the Law and were ostracized by the orthodox Jewish community.

Not only did Jesus enlist Levi as a disciple, but he also ate in his house with other "sinners and tax-collectors." The Pharisees were scandalized by this.

"Why does he eat with tax-collectors and sinners?" they asked the other disciples.

Jesus heard the question.

"Those who are well have no need of a physician, but those who are sick," he said. "I came not to call the righteous, but sinners" (Mark 2:17).

As his ministry was to prove, there was a touch of facetiousness in this remark. The Pharisees were anything but righteous, and the persons they regarded as sinners were not necessarily the real unrighteous ones.

Then there was the matter of sabbatarianism—or

127

extremely strict observance of the Sabbath—which had been carried by the Pharisees to the point of absurdity. People could not drag chairs across the floor on the Sabbath, for the making of a furrow in the dirt, however slight, was considered to be "plowing." Mothers could not carry their children on the Sabbath, for to do so would be to "carry a burden."

Jesus took issue with the tradition on two occasions; first, over plucking grain (Mark 2:23-28; Matthew 12:1-8) and second over healing (Mark 3:16; Matthew 12:9-14).

His disciples pulled the heads off some grain as they passed through a field and probably ground them in their hands, as country people did, to separate the wheat from the chaff. This occurred on a Sabbath, and the Pharisees were incensed at this infraction of the highly codified Law. Jesus, unperturbed, pointed out to them that David and his men had once eaten the consecrated bread of the temple, which only priests were supposed to eat, because they were hungry and in need. "The sabbath was made for man," he said, "not man for the sabbath" (Mark 2:27).

Ernst Käsemann was probably right in calling this the most revolutionary thing Jesus ever said. It turned the whole world of Hebrew legalism on its head.

When Jesus entered the synagogue on the Sabbath, the Pharisees were watching to see if he would heal a man with a withered hand. The very fact that they were thus engaged is an indictment of their spirit. When Jesus saw the man with the afflicted hand, he did not hesitate. "Come here," he commanded the man. "Is it lawful on the sabbath," he asked the Pharisees, "to do good or to do harm, to save life or to kill?" (Mark 3:4) They were silent before such a piercing question. Jesus looked at them "with anger, grieved at their hardness of heart," and healed the man.

Immediately, says Mark, the Pharisees went out and began plotting with the Herodians about "how to destroy him." The entire conflict that led to the crucifixion, in other words, began over Jesus' attitude toward the Sabbath. He staked his whole life and ministry on a liberal, generous understanding of the commandments. God had not given the Jewish people a bitter medicine to swallow with reluctance; God had given them a prescription for joy and grace. The scribes and Pharisees had turned blessing into bane and freedom into bondage. They had used the letter of the Law to focus attention on the wrong things and to avoid "the weightier matters" of life.

II. Jesus' Teaching

Much of Jesus' *teaching*, as well as the personal example of his life, was devoted to correcting the general misunderstanding of the Law.

Matthew 15 is a case in point. Jesus is chided by the scribes and Pharisees because his disciples do not wash their hands before eating, to fulfill the ceremonial law about cleansing. Jesus responds vigorously, counterattacking these self-righteous men as mere lip-religionists, not true pietists. They profess to follow the commandment about honoring father and mother, yet manage through a neat legal trick not to give their parents financial assistance when they need it. Their trick is to declare their extra money "corban," or dedicated to God, so that it may not be touched for human use.

The truth about the legalists, says Jesus, was spoken by the prophet Isaiah:

> This people honors me with their
> lips,
> but their heart is far from me;
> in vain do they worship me,
> teaching as doctrines the precepts
> of men.
>
> (Mark 7:6-7)

It isn't what enters the mouth that defiles a person, Jesus teaches the crowds, but what comes out of the mouth—that is, lies, deceits, vanities, and hypocrisies.

Matthew then relates the account of Jesus' ministering to a Canaanite woman whose daughter is ill. At first he demurs, in good Jewish fashion, because she is not one of the chosen people. Then he relents because of her insistent faith.

Finally, in the same chapter, Jesus feeds a multitude of people in the wilderness because he has compassion on them. He has been teaching on the mountainside and healing the blind, lame, maimed, and dumb. And when they become hungry, he feeds them—presumably without ceremonial cleansing! It is a banquet of the *am ha 'aretz*, the people of the land, who are all regarded as sinners by the self-righteous scribes and Pharisees.

What has happened, Jesus sees, is that the scribes and Pharisees have missed the whole point of the Law, which was to produce a nation of God's people who loved and cared for one another.

When Jesus is asked to name the most important commandment of all, he responds that it is to love God with all one's heart, soul, mind, and strength, and then to love one's neighbor as oneself (Mark 12:28-34; Matthew 22:34-40; Luke 10:25-28). Love, in other words, is the whole intention of the Law. No matter how punctilious the scribes and Pharisees were in observing the letter of the Law, it was all futile unless they did so in a spirit of peace and good will.

In the Lucan version of this teaching, Jesus adds the famous story of the good Samaritan (Luke 10:29-37). The point of the story, which must have had enormous impact on an audience of scribes and Pharisees, is that the Samaritan, who by legal definition is a sinner and an unrighteous person, is the one person in the story who fulfills God's Law of love. The priest and Levite who pass by on the other side of the road because of their legalistic points of view are exactly like the scribes and Pharisees: they have missed the real significance of the Law in their passion to observe its letter!

Because the religious leaders of the time could not tolerate the truth Jesus brought to bear upon their framework of lies and hypocrisy, they eventually orchestrated his crucifixion at the hands of the Romans, adding to their history of guilt by dishonoring the commandment against bearing false witness. Again and again, in the various trials that culminated in Jesus' death, they insisted on stories of his disloyalty to Rome, which were simply untrue.

III. Jesus' Messiahship of Obedience

But God, who is a God of truth and justice, would not permit the evil to win so definitive a battle, and crowned the Messiahship of his faithful teacher by raising him from death and establishing his ministry in a new, transcendent dimension. The pouring out of his Spirit, confirmed by the experience of the early Christians at Pentecost, enabled the followers of Jesus to live under the commandments with great joy and vitality.

The center of the new kingdom was love, the love of God and love of neighbor, which Jesus had said is the real focus of the commandments. On the evening before his death, in a fellowship meal foreshadowing the banqueting of the kingdom itself, Jesus said to his disciples, "This is my commandment, that you love one another as I have loved you" (John 15:12). Following his resurrection, he appeared to the disciples, including the shamed and fallen Peter, at the Sea of Galilee, and asked Peter, "Simon, son of John, do you love me?" (John 21:15, 16, 17). It was a strange question from the Messiah of the world. Yet it was most appropriate, given the framework of his understanding, his perception that all commandments, and therefore all obedience, find their natural center in love. He might have asked Peter, "Peter, will you obey me now?" Instead, he struck to the very heart of the matter, and asked whether Peter loved him. If Peter did, there would be no question about the obedience.

The same is always true of our following the commandments. If we love God and our neighbors, there is no question about our behavior. The Law is not abrogated by Christ's coming, as the television preacher suggested; it is merely set in its true perspective.

Appendix II

Paul and the Commandments

Kenneth Bailey, director of the international center for biblical studies at Tantur, Israel, confessed once in a lecture that for years he did not consider Jesus to be a theologian. Paul, he knew, was a great theologian, and among the apostles so were John and Peter. But Jesus he simply dismissed as a preacher who did not think conceptually.

"Then one day it hit me," he said, "that Jesus was a *metaphorical* theologian, one who thought in pictures and images. Paul, on the other hand, was an *academic* theologian who had been trained in the Greek manner and thought systematically about problems. Paul took the theological system developed by Jesus, transformed it into academic theology, and laid the foundation for the entire Christian epoch."

Whether or not one agrees with Dr. Bailey's distinction between metaphorical and academic theology, there can be little disagreement about his assessment of Paul's role in Christian history. No other preacher, teacher, or writer has held such a central place in the development of Christian thought and understanding.

Paul's dramatic encounter with the risen Christ

on the road to Damascus was a pivotal experience in his life. From his childhood, he had been a zealous Pharisee—"a Pharisee of the Pharisees," he once termed himself. Devotion to the commandments was the most important thing in his existence. When he first learned about Jesus and his followers as men who set themselves above or outside the practices of the Pharisees, he must have considered them the most threatening heretics of the age, capable of undermining and even destroying the greatest traditions of the religious life. Eventually he joined the struggle to eradicate the "heretics." With all the fierce energy that would later make him a key figure in establishing Christian missions, he began a determined and systematic effort to rid the world of such radical antinomians.

Along the way to this ambition, however, something obviously happened to Paul. In his enthusiasm to destroy Christianity from the face of the earth, he undoubtedly learned everything he could about it. What he learned began to seep through the armor of his mind, challenging his dearest conceptions. What if Jesus were right, that love was more important than the individual commandments? Had not Paul himself been occasionally disgusted with the fusty old Pharisees, who strutted about in their self-righteousness as if they owned the world? Didn't God often side with the underdogs in a fight like this?

Paul's conversion experience on the way to Damascus was most likely not a sudden, unexpected event but the climax of a desperate inner struggle. "Saul, Saul," said Jesus, using his Hebrew name, "why do you persecute me?" (Acts 9:4). Perhaps Paul had been under the growing conviction that what he was doing was wrong, that he was actually persecuting the memory of one of God's true prophets.

In that strange moment along the road, a great upheaval finally took place in Paul's life. The truth got the upper hand at last, and his brief period of psychosomatic blindness was symbolic of what a gigantic turnover had occurred in his personality. Thinking he saw, he realized he didn't, and his eyes had to be anointed by a messenger of God before he could see the world from a completely new perspective.

For the remainder of his life, Paul would preach from the energy of this radically new perspective that had forced its way into his experience. In one sense, especially among his Jewish brethren, his entire message would proceed from a different understanding of the place of the commandments in the scheme of things. The Law kills, he would say, but the Spirit gives life.

Paul's entire theology can be summed up under seven categorical statements, all of which are derived from his changed understanding of the Law:

(1) *It is impossible to keep the commandments without error.* Human flesh, in and of itself, is weak and fails even as it believes it is succeeding. Surely,

Paul boasted, no one had more reason for confidence in the flesh than he: "circumcised on the eighth day, of the people of Israel, of the tribe of Benjamin, a Hebrew born of Hebrews; as to the law a Pharisee, as to zeal a persecutor of the church, as to righteousness under the law blameless" (Philippians 3:5-6). But what Paul came to see, and what all intelligent persons ought to recognize, is that having a moral code does not, in and of itself, give us the power to live by it. There are darker forces at work in us. "I do not understand my own actions," Paul wrote to the Romans. "For I do not do what I want, but I do the very thing I hate. . . . I can will what is right, but I cannot do it. For I do not do the good I want, but the evil I do not want is what I do" (Romans 7:15, 18-19). This is the moral confession of one of the most respected Pharisees of his time. The commandments, he said, are good, but there is an evil force inside us that often triumphs over them.

(2) *For this reason, the commandments God gave for our edification have become the occasion of our condemnation.* If we believe we shall be justified before God by obeying them, we are wrong. Such a spirit leads only to pride and arrogance in our hearts, which can be a greater evil than the sins we avoid by observing the commandments. Moreover, reliance on our own righteousness, and not on the righteousness of God, leads to an accursed condition. "For all who rely on works of the law are under a curse; for it is written, 'Cursed be every one who does not abide by all things written in the book of

137

the law, and do them'" (Galatians 3:10). No one escapes this condemnation, because "all have sinned and fall short of the glory of God" (Romans 3:23).

(3) *Jesus was right, love is more important than the Law, and it is the heart God judges, not the apparent behavior of a person.* God gave the commandments as helpful guides, but our sinful natures twisted and abused even these. Now God has sent his Son to reveal this and to show us a better way. The Law was our custodian or teacher until Christ came. Under the Law, we were "no better than a slave" (Galatians 4:1), obliged to follow rules we did not understand. But Christ has shown us the Father and established our full standing as his children, and because we are his children, "God has sent the Spirit of his Son into our hearts, crying, 'Abba! Father!'" (Galatians 4:6)

(4) *Jesus' death on the cross is the great example of God's love and good will toward us as his children.* "While we were still weak, Christ died for the ungodly" (Romans 5:6). "God shows his love for us in that while we were yet sinners Christ died for us" (Romans 5:8). Christ redeemed us from the curse of sin by himself becoming a curse, "For it is written, 'Cursed be every one who hangs on a tree'" (Galatians 3:13). God "canceled the bond which stood against us"—the statement of our indebtedness to sin—"nailing it to the cross" (Colossians 2:14). The overwhelming effect of Christ's ministry, his teachings, and his subsequent death by

crucifixion was to assure us that God loves and cares for us as a father loves and cares for his true children, and that we are to live in that love and care as free persons, not as fearful slaves to an impossible system of rules and regulations.

(5) *The resurrection of Jesus is the most dramatic example of the power of a new Spirit at work in us and the world.* Paul knew that Jesus lives; he had met him on the road to Damascus. He also saw that this extraordinary phenomenon, of a dead man's being raised up and appearing to others, divided all time and history. A new era had begun, in which God's Spirit was being poured out liberally on all who would accept the truth and live by it. If none of this is true, he said, and Christ was not raised, then "Your faith is futile and you are still in your sins" (I Corinthians 15:17). Our victory over legalism depends on the resurrection and this new Spirit at work in the world.

(6)*The Spirit enables us to keep the commandments and to go beyond them in love and sacrifice.* Now, "We serve not under the old written code but in the new life of the Spirit" (Romans 7:6). God sent his Son among us so that we might walk "not according to the flesh but according to the Spirit" (Romans 8:4). The very desires of our hearts are different under the Spirit, and we no longer yearn for the things that are against the commandments. We are, therefore, "ministers of a new covenant, not in a written code but in the Spirit; for the written code kills, but the Spirit gives life" (II Corinthians 3:6).

Unspiritual persons cannot understand this, for they have not received the gifts of the Spirit. However, the spiritual person understands perfectly, judging all things, while he himself is "judged by no one," having in him "the mind of Christ" (I Corinthians 2:15-16). The secret is in the heart of the spiritual person. You should give thanks to God, said Paul, that you who were once the slaves of sin "have become obedient from the heart to the standard of teaching to which you were committed" and have thus become the slaves of righteousness (Romans 6:17). The commandments are in no way abrogated, but now, in the Spirit of God, we can be obedient with real enthusiasm!

(7) *Because the foregoing is true, we should all seek to live more and more in love and forgiveness, and to bring the blessing of Christ to the world.* In his great prayer for the church in Ephesians 3:14-19, Paul asked "that Christ may dwell in your hearts through faith; that you, being rooted and grounded in love, may have power to comprehend with all the saints what is the breadth and length and height and depth, and to know the love of Christ which surpasses knowledge, that you may be filled with all the fullness of God." For the Philippians, he asked "that your love may abound more and more, with knowledge and all discernment, so that you may approve what is excellent, and may be pure and blameless for the day of Christ, filled with the fruits of righteousness which come through Jesus Christ, to the glory and praise of God" (Philippians 1:9-11).

And to the Corinthians, of course, he wrote the great hymn to love in I Corinthians 13.

If I speak with the eloquence of men and of angels, but have no love, I become no more than blaring brass or crashing cymbal. If I have the gift of foretelling the future and hold in my mind not only all human knowledge but the very secrets of God, and if I also have that absolute faith which can move mountains, but have no love, I amount to nothing at all. If I dispose of all that I possess, yes, even if I give my own body to be burned, but have no love, I achieve precisely nothing.

This love of which I speak is slow to lose patience—it looks for a way of being constructive. It is not possessive: it is neither anxious to impress nor does it cherish inflated ideas of its own importance.

Love has good manners and does not pursue selfish advantage. It is not touchy. It does not keep account of evil or gloat over the wickedness of other people. On the contrary, it shares the joy of those who live by the truth.

Love knows no limit to its endurance, no end to its trust, no fading of its hope; it can outlast anything. Love never fails.

For if there are prophecies they will be fulfilled and done with, if there are "tongues" the need for them will disappear, if there is knowledge it will be swallowed up in truth. For our knowledge is always incomplete and our prophecy is always incomplete, and when the complete comes, that is the end of the incomplete.

When I was a little child I talked and felt and thought like a little child. Now that I am a man I have finished with childish things.

At present we are men looking at puzzling reflections in a

mirror. The time will come when we shall see reality whole and face to face! At present all I know is a little fraction of the truth, but the time will come when I shall know it as fully as God has known me!

In this life we have three lasting qualities—faith, hope, and love. But the greatest of them is love. (JBP)

What Paul came to understand is the inadequacy of human flesh to live solely by the commandments. The commandments were a gift of God to lead us to new understanding. But with the understanding came the realization of our inadequacy. We need more; we need the very Spirit of God to live by the ways of God. So God sent his Son to teach us the ways of his Spirit, and then imparted his Spirit to enable us to live in a new dimension.

Paul was fond of describing the whole matter in terms of slavery and freedom. When he finally arrived at the realization that he had been enslaved by sin through the commandments, he experienced the great freedom of being in Christ. Then he liked to think of himself as a new kind of slave—Christ's slave. He gladly considered himself a slave of this new Master, for Christ had manumitted him from a horrible bondage.

"Thanks be to God," he wrote to his friends in Corinth, "who continually leads us about, captives in Christ's triumphal procession, and everywhere uses us to reveal and spread abroad the fragrance of the knowledge of himself!" (II Corinthians 2:14 NEB). The image is one of a conquering general leading his captives in chains behind him. "How wonderful," Paul was saying, "to belong to this new Master!"

Paul still cared deeply for the Law. He was always conservative in dealing with converts, to be sure that they understood that they were not free from moral dictates. But he held the Law in a revised perspective, as the gift of a God whose love goes far beyond any legal arrangement.

"I through the law died to the law," he told the Galatians, "that I might live to God. I have been crucified with Christ; it is no longer I who live, but Christ who lives in me; and the life I now live in the flesh I live by faith in the Son of God, who loved me and gave himself for me" (Galatians 2:19-20).

His identification with Christ on the matter of the Law was so complete that he felt as if he had gone to the cross with Christ, and now lived in and through him. And it was all possible because of the great love that had overshadowed the Law!